Take 5! for Language Arts

Writing that builds critical-thinking skills (K–2)

BY KAYE HAGLER

T0308405

MAUPIN HOUSE BY
CAPSTONE PROFESSIONAL
a capstone imprint

Take 5! for Language Arts: Writing that builds critical-thinking skills (K–2)

By Kaye Hagler
© Copyright 2017. Kaye Hagler. All rights reserved.

Cover Design: Charmaine Whitman
Book Design: Charmaine Whitman and Lisa King

Library of Congress Cataloging-in-Publication Data
Names: Hagler, Kaye R., author.
Title: Take 5! for language arts : writing that builds critical-thinking
    skills (K-2) / by Kaye Hagler.
Other titles: Take five for language arts
Description: North Mankato, MN : Maupin House Publishing, Inc. by Capstone
    Professional, 2017. | Includes bibliographical references and index.
Identifiers: LCCN 2016023653| ISBN 9781496608086 (pbk.) | ISBN 9781496608093
    (eBook PDF) | ISBN 9781496608109 (eBook)
Subjects: LCSH: Language arts (Elementary)—Activity programs. | Language
    arts (Elementary)—Audio-visual aids. | Critical thinking—Study and
    teaching (Elementary)—Activity programs. | Critical thinking—Study and
    teaching (Elementary)—Audio-visual aids. | English language—Study and
    teaching (Elementary)—Audio-visual aids. | Teaching—Aids and devices.
Classification: LCC LB1576 .H213 2017 | DDC 372.4—dc23
LC record available at https://lccn.loc.gov/2016023653

Image Credits:
Shutterstock: Andre Adams, 192 (bottom fish), Andrey Makurin, 108 (deer), Andrey Oleynik, 139, arbit, 157 (middle), Artur. B, 76 (buildings), Atomic Roderick, 20 (right), Atstock Productions, 22, BlueRingMedia, 143, browndogstudios, 76 (taxi), cartoons, 156 (right), Cory Thoman, 192 (middle left), Danomyte, 157 (bottom), Denys Koltovskyi, 122, Elinorka, 192 (bottom seaweed), GraphicsRF, 28, Ho Yeow Hui, 191 (plane), Ihnatovich Maryia, 133, Irmun, 8, iunewind, 47, jehsomwang, 32, Ken Benner, 46, 153, Kostenyukova Nataliya, 108 (faces), Lanteria, 21, lineartestpilot, 158, Lorelyn Medina, 53, Lubenica, 19 (top), Macrovector, 76 (hospital), mhatzapa, 48, 188 (border), Mikhaylova Anna, 192 (bottom left), popocorn, 154, Potapov Alexander, 108 (paw prints), Pushkin, 60, Ramcreativ, 108 (footprints), Rangsan Paidaen, 166, Regular, 157 (top), RetroClipArt, 20 (left), Sarawut Padungkwan, 49, schwarzhana, 192 (top left), Seamartini Graphics, 108 (tent), SlipFloat, 108 (mountains), Studio Barcelona, 105, Supza, 108 (sun), Tomacco, 106, veron_ice, 191 (weather symbols), Volyk Ievgenii, 76 (tree), What's My Name, 163, Wong Salam, 131, Yayayoyo, 156 (left), Yoko Design, 76 (park), Zhe Vasylieva, 36, zizi_mentos, 19 (bottom), Zoran Milic, 110

Capstone Professional publishes professional resources for K–12 educators. Contact us for tailored, in-school training or to schedule an author for a workshop or conference. Visit www.capstonepd.com for free lesson plan downloads.

This book includes websites that were operational at the time this book went to press.

Maupin House Publishing, Inc. by Capstone Professional
1710 Roe Crest Drive
North Mankato, MN 56003
www.capstonepd.com
888-262-6135
info@capstonepd.com

Table of Contents

Introduction:
Beginning the Take 5! Adventure

"Take five!" the director calls, and everyone is so relieved. They have been working on the set for hours and need a break.

"Take five!" the conductor announces; immediately the musicians stand and stretch. They have been practicing for hours, rehearsing for the upcoming concert, and their muscles need a break.

"Let's take five!" the teacher calls to the class, and everyone is excited. They have been waiting for this time of the day when elephants, fairy tale kingdoms, and zoo animals come to life on the page. All are ready to create, describe, draw, defend, question, share, and play—and that is the expectation of *Take 5! for Language Arts*. Students never know what new adventure may lie ahead, so their pencils and journals or laptops are out and ready. This is a welcome break, one that provides a unique opportunity each day for creative and critical thinking.

The first *Take 5! for Language Arts* has become a standard for writing in classrooms all over the world. The edition from 2012 continues to energize and challenge students in the upper grades. One day, however, while preparing for an upcoming session at a writing conference, a teacher approached me.

"I teach first graders. So when are you going to write one for my students? They need these same challenges."

The book you are now reading answers that question. Now is the time for even beginning writers to "take five!"

Where better to foster "a community of writers" (Bratcher, 2009) than in those first years in the classroom?

Chapter One:
Fostering a Writing Environment

Writing Begins One Step at a Time

The process of writing, of associating sounds with letters and letters with words, is a gradual one. This process requires students to accomplish a series of steps that culminates in the formation of sentences. This step-by-step process, however, does not always take into account the content of what is written, the voice, or the motivation for writing in the first place. *Take 5! for Language Arts* aims to get students excited about the writing process and see writing as an opportunity for discovering self, for developing ideas, and for sharing those ideas with others. With this approach, students will encounter problems to solve. They will be dazzled by a narrative prompt that will take them into another place and time. They will find themselves taking a stand on an issue and asserting that claim with reasons. And all of this is possible as early as the kindergarten years because these students do have ideas, opinions, and information to share. They just need a framework for all those words to come bubbling to the surface and onto the page. That is what *Take 5! for Language Arts* is all about.

In this introduction, classroom discussion questions are provided for setting the foundation for a writing program. I also stress the teacher's many roles in this program as the writing facilitator. So what does an effective writing facilitator do?

- emphasizes that writing enables students to build important connections to self, to others, and to the text.
- provides purpose for student writing.
- establishes a dynamic and challenging environment for writing.
- maintains a well-stocked writing lab or workshop.

Together, the following four practices will allow students to embrace the writing workshop as an opportunity for discovery. Additionally, questions for students and teachers are provided for stimulating conversations about writing.

Classroom Discussion Question:

What do you remember about your first writing experiences?

Building Connections

As soon as words go onto a screen or page, a connection is being made:

- a connection to self
- a connection to others
- a connection to text

Another way to look at these connections is that they are part of *communication*, or the sharing of information, ideas, or opinions. However, this communication needs to be clear for others to understand it. "The goal of writing instruction should be for students to be facile at developing sentences and extending text that clearly conveys meaning and reflects the writer's intentions as well" (Graham & Hebert, 2010).

Writing is our way of communicating with others and with ourselves. It allows all those frustrations, joys, bubbling ideas, and concerns to come to the surface and be represented through words on the page, and those words should be meaningfully constructed and organized. Most important of all, writing serves a meaningful purpose. That is the message for our students.

Classroom Discussion Question:

What are some ways we can share our ideas, opinions, creativity, and feelings with other people through writing?

Establishing Purpose

Excitement can be contagious, and writing is an exciting part of the language arts curriculum as it gives students many opportunities to explore their own interests and ideas. Writing sharpens students' critical thinking, spurs their creative juices, and provides a platform for their concerns and ideas. As numerous studies have shown, writing on a regular basis increases writing ability. "Students need to write frequently and regularly to become comfortable with writing, to develop their ideas as they write, and to further hone their skills as writers" (Graham, MacArthur & Fitzgerald, 2013).

In their first experience with writing, children begin to discover the many forms of communication print offers. They see grocery lists, signs along the road, print material in the home, e-mails and texts, labels on grocery products, sticky notes on the refrigerator, letters, and greeting cards. As emerging writers, they begin to sense different purposes for writing. They know a note on the refrigerator serves as a reminder for a task or that a book brings pleasure as a story unfolds.

As students become more proficient in writing, their exposure to writing purposes becomes more important. Will the purpose be to write a narrative, or story, about a fun adventure? Will the purpose be to state an opinion, to provide information, or to describe a place visited on vacation? "Since writers outside school have many different purposes beyond demonstrating accountability and they use more diverse genres of writing, it is important that students have experiences within school that teach them how writing differs with purpose, audience, and other elements" (NCTE, 2016). Authentic writing opportunities can help students better grasp the many choices available to them in independent writing. "Teachers will need to provide challenging materials that require children to analyze and think creatively and from different points of view ... to analyze topics, generate questions, and organize written responses for different purposes in meaningful activities" (NAEYC, 1998).

Students' experiences can become an important beginning for discovering writing opportunities. As noted educator and writer Lucy Calkins explains, "This is how I write. I take a moment—an image, a memory, a phrase, an idea—and I hold it in my hands and declare it a treasure" (Calkins, 1994). As teachers, it is our task to lead students toward discovering the many treasures lurking in their minds. This can happen through questioning and through modeling the process of finding a purpose in writing.

Classroom Discussion Question:

Where can words be found in your home? What are their purposes?

Creating a Dynamic and Challenging Learning Environment

The word *dynamic* means *changing* or *progressing*. A dynamic writing environment is one that both changes and challenges students to progress to newer, deeper levels. As Peter Johnston puts it, "Teaching is planned opportunism" (2012). The teacher makes available resources that can spur independent writing opportunities. A typical dynamic classroom, for instance, would include many of the following elements for writing instruction:

- a word wall that is updated throughout the school year, reflecting changing topics, situations, and ideas encountered in authentic classroom experiences
- a well-equipped writing center
- anchor charts along the wall that reinforce writing mini-lessons (see pp. 189–192)
- a variety of books and pictures to stimulate thinking (fiction, nonfiction, and poetry)
- software for publishing and designing a variety of student-produced products
- clearly labeled equipment, learning centers, supplies, and objects around the room (shelves, books, screens)
- wall strips, clotheslines, bulletin boards, or other means for displaying student writing and products
- listening stations with audiobooks and headphones
- large, easy-to-read signs that communicate information (lunch schedules, calendars, classroom helpers, etc.)

Classroom Discussion Question:

What areas in our classroom could provide additional writing opportunities?

Maintaining a Well-stocked Writing Center

One of those little rewards in teaching came the day I sat and watched a student walk over to a table in my small classroom and pull a sheet of yellow construction paper from the basket. Curious, I watched as he then waded through a bucket of markers until he found the one he wanted. He then pulled out a chair and began, totally focused on his task.

As I walked around the classroom, I paused by his side and saw the card he was creating. He smiled and looked up. His mom had just had a baby that week, a baby brother for him, and he wanted to make her a card. Those few dollars I spent on supplies were worth every penny to me at that moment. My student had a purpose, and my small writing center made that purpose possible. From that moment on, I became a garage sale demon, looking for small buckets, photography books, old packs of crayons, buttons, rulers, ribbons, and even old plastic jewelry containers to store small items. The following is a list of items that might work well in your writing center.

❑ Assorted writing paper, both lined and unlined, plain and decorated
❑ Colored pencils
❑ Construction paper
❑ Embellishments for greetings cards or journals
❑ Envelopes
❑ Glue sticks
❑ Greetings cards with the backs removed
❑ Hole punch
❑ Markers
❑ Wallpaper samples
❑ Peel-off labels
❑ Pencils
❑ Pencil sharpener
❑ Pens
❑ Photographs
❑ Plastic bins to organize materials
❑ Rulers
❑ Small note pads (businesses often have extras of these)
❑ Stamps and ink pads
❑ Stickers
❑ Sticky notes
❑ Tape
❑ Yarn and string for binding books

Parents and friends can often be called upon to help stock a writing center with materials already on hand.

Chapter Two:

How to Use Take 5!: Seven Key Components

The prompts in this book are written to support critical language arts skills. Along with the Language Link, each prompt corresponds with six other key components for instruction: the Learning Setting, Depth of Knowledge (or level of difficulty), Supplies, Standards written as ability statements, Prompts, and Let's Explore More (lesson extensions). The prompts in *Take 5!* allow teachers to make crucial decisions for the needs of each day. If, for instance, teachers need reinforcement for narrative writing or capitalization, a quick glance at the Index (pp. 12–17) will help them locate an appropriate prompt. Prompts may be used as an introduction, continued practice, or review of a literacy link. Be prepared for repeat sessions with some of your students' favorite prompts.

Breaking Down Each Prompt: Seven Key Components

Take a look at the prompt example provided to clearly see the breakdown of each prompt. Each component is clearly labeled and explained on the pages that follow.

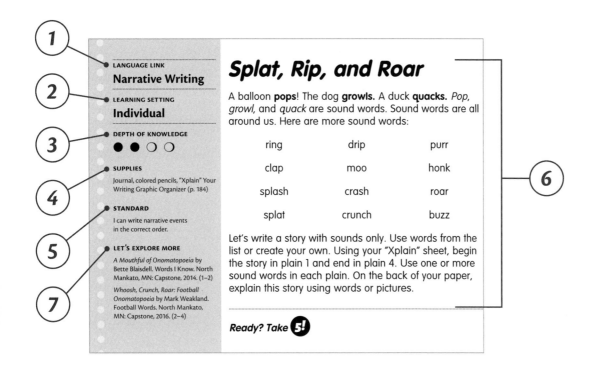

LANGUAGE LINK
Narrative Writing

LEARNING SETTING
Individual

DEPTH OF KNOWLEDGE
● ● ○ ○

SUPPLIES
Journal, colored pencils, "Xplain" Your Writing Graphic Organizer (p. 184)

STANDARD
I can write narrative events in the correct order.

LET'S EXPLORE MORE
A Mouthful of Onomatopoeia by Bette Blaisdell. Words I Know. North Mankato, MN: Capstone, 2014. (1–2)

Whoosh, Crunch, Roar: Football Onomatopoeia by Mark Weakland. Football Words. North Mankato, MN: Capstone, 2016. (2–4)

Splat, Rip, and Roar

A balloon **pops**! The dog **growls**. A duck **quacks**. *Pop, growl,* and *quack* are sound words. Sound words are all around us. Here are more sound words:

ring	drip	purr
clap	moo	honk
splash	crash	roar
splat	crunch	buzz

Let's write a story with sounds only. Use words from the list or create your own. Using your "Xplain" sheet, begin the story in plain 1 and end in plain 4. Use one or more sound words in each plain. On the back of your paper, explain this story using words or pictures.

Ready? Take **5!**

(1) **Language Link**—This is the skill area correlated with a standard (informative writing, spelling, punctuation, etc.). See pages 168–174 for a list of all links and corresponding standards.

(2) **Learning Setting**—While most prompts are geared toward individual writing experiences, others call for paired or collaborative (small group) settings. For the latter two, teachers can assign partners and groups or use something similar to a partner pail, which is a container filled with student names. The teacher pulls two, four, or five names from the pail (depending on the learning setting needed) to establish groups. Teachers may also use a program such as the Random Group Generator in Google Docs to automatically generate a list of students in groups.

(3) **Depth of Knowledge**—Norman Webb's Depth of Knowledge Levels (DOK) is a schema that assigns a number from one to four for the cognitive expectation, or depth of knowledge, needed for a given task. The system moves from recall of information, a Level 1 skill, to higher levels of critical thinking at Level 4. "The model is based upon the assumption that curricular elements may all be categorized based upon the cognitive demands required to produce an acceptable response. Each grouping of tasks reflects a different level of cognitive expectation, or depth of knowledge, required to complete the task" (Albuquerque Public Schools, 2016). The levels are as follows:

Level 1: Recall and Reproduction

Level 2: Skills and Concepts

Level 3: Strategic Thinking

Level 4: Extended Thinking

A helpful PDF pamphlet with the complete breakdown of the four levels can be found on the Albuquerque Public Schools website.

(4) **Supplies**—These items are needed for students to complete each prompt. Teachers should have these ready for the students to use the day of the given prompt. Most important of all is the journal. Some may call it a *writing notebook, response journal,* or *reflective journal. Take 5! for Language Arts* refers to it as simply the *journal.* A paper journal and pencil are the default supplies for writing, but a journal can also be a folder on the computers that students use. It may be a spiral-bound composition book or a binder with loose-leaf paper. It can even be half sheets of paper that are bound together.

(5) **Standards and Ability Statements**—The Common Core College and Career Readiness Standards are used for the prompts, and the Alphabetical Index of Prompts starting on page 168 provides the standards correlations for the prompts. However, each prompt is also paired with one or more ability statements. These "I can" learning objectives frame the standard to be mastered in language easily understood by the student. "Students can't see, recognize, and understand what they need to learn until we translate the learning intention into developmentally appropriate, student-friendly, and culturally respectful language" (Zimmerman, 2001).

As many teachers have found, a long, often complex standard displayed in the classroom (as required by many schools) is a guide more for the teachers and evaluators who visit the classroom than it is for the students. It does not "matter what we decide students need to learn, not much will happen until students understand what they are supposed to learn during a lesson and set their sights on learning it" (Moss, Brookhart, and Long, 2011). Therefore, the "I can," or ability, statements provide a specific learning target that helps shift the responsibility of learning back to the student. These statements are successfully used in many classrooms and help students more directly understand what they need to learn.

Compare the difference:

"I can" statement:
I can support my opinion with reasons.

Complete Standard:
W.2.1. Write opinion pieces in which they introduce the topic or book they are writing about, state an opinion, supply reasons that support the opinion, use linking words (e.g., because, and, also) to connect opinion and reasons, and provide a concluding statement or section.

The third-person pronoun "they" in the W.2.1 standard often alienates the student from the standard. However, the first-person pronoun "I" in the ability statement makes a personal connection to the student.

(6) **Prompt**—Prompts appear as independent activities, as modeling and practice exercises in the mini-lessons, and as additional Let's Explore More activities, which appear on prompt pages as well.

(7) **Let's Explore More**—These are extensions of the lessons offering additional resources, including books, websites, prompt extensions, or topic-related activities.

Displaying the Prompts

Teachers have various options for delivery. Three main options have worked well for teachers who have successfully implemented *Take 5! for Language Arts* in the upper grade levels. Visual displays should always accompany the prompts, but at the K–2 level, verbal directions are important guides for the writing prompt. Three possible display options for the prompts include:

- Interactive whiteboards or a projector
- Individual paper copies for each student
- Handwritten instructions on the board for shorter prompts

Responding to Prompts

Most prompts allow students to write or draw their responses in their journals. Drawing can provide many opportunities for beginning writers. Drawing helps them visualize thinking as writing a complete thought may be beyond reach. Drawing should begin with a pencil first and details with color added later. As a wise first-grade teacher once said, "If their illustrations are detailed, their writing can be detailed as well."

Several graphic organizers have been provided to help students organize their thinking. A large "Xplain" Your Writing Graphic Organizer (p. 184) is often referred to in the prompts for students to "explain" their ideas. Essentially, it is a grid in the form of an X that allows students to add their ideas to each plain, or space. They can also just make a large X on a page in their journal.

Though the prompts are quick writes, suitable for a small amount of time each day, writing guides are also provided. Many of the prompts are appropriate for later development into essay form, following the steps of the writing process. These guides serve as road maps to students' writing development and can help students focus their writing each step of the way from topic selection, essay development, and peer editing to assessment. Guides can be glued or taped into the journal when finished. Additionally, they can be made into posters and used as anchor charts for the classroom. The following writing guides are included starting on page 186:

- A Writer's Checklist
- My Writing Page
- Let's Write About
- ABC Writing Chart
- Peer Conference Guide
- Journal Rubric for Developing Writers
- Journal Rubric for Beginning Writers

Sharing Responses

Sharing responses is an important learning opportunity for students. Following each session, students should be encouraged to share their responses with the class. Some students are always eager to share what they have written, so sharing is no problem. Others will begin to participate more when they see the level of acceptance given to all ideas. For visual responses, a place in the classroom can accommodate the products of students' thinking/discovering sessions. Many popular apps and websites allow students to create their own stories by choosing preset settings and characters or even creating their own. Many apps, however, tend to upgrade (with accompanying glitches), be discontinued, or gradually build add-in purchases for full use of the app. For these reasons, few apps are listed under the Let's Explore More section. When desired, teachers, can easily find many versions of these story makers by searching online.

Assessing the Prompts

The process of encouraging students to think critically and creatively can come to a screeching halt if a big red N ("needs improvement") appears on a student's paper. A cute stamp on the page is always a good way to encourage thinking as is a colorful check mark. A nod, a "good job," and other informal feedback also work well. The two rubrics provided on pages 191 and 192 are for developing writers and beginning writers.

As mentioned earlier, these are useful for extended writing opportunities when prompts such as those for opinion writing are revisited for a full writing assignment. These informal assessments are helpful in learning the progress students have made in their formal writing ability, generally on a monthly basis. The self-assessment in the Journal Rubric for Beginning Writers (page 192) can help students independently track their own progress, along with writing skills that need to be strengthened.

This framework for a regular routine of writing allows teachers, parents, and students to discover the changes that can take place over the course of one school year. The journal allows students to take writing steps before moving forward, which deepens their range of writing ability and expression as they find just the right words for a given response as they connect, then communicate.

Ready to begin? Let's Take 5! *for Language Arts!*

Index to Prompts as They Appear in the Book

(Alphabetical Index of Prompts can be found on pp. 168–174)

Prompt	Language Link	Learning Setting	Page
Splat, Rip, and Roar	Narrative Writing	Individual	40
Kings Bree and McFee	Antonyms	Individual	41
Letter Swap	Spelling Patterns	Individual	42
The Very Verby Vacation	Verbs	Individual	43
Bottleplants and Eggtrees	Compound Words	Collaborative	44
A Peachy Preposition	Prepositions Narrative Writing	Individual	45
Watch Out, Nate!	Prepositions Narrative Writing	Pair	45
Bad News for Bears	Interrogatives	Individual	46
The Rest of the Story	Research	Individual	46
Book Report	Opinion Writing	Individual	47
A Day at the Beach	Opinion Writing	Individual	48
The Quiet Thief	Plural Nouns	Individual	49
Fear in the Forest	Plural Nouns	Individual	50
Puppy Doctor	Informative Writing	Individual	51
Treasure or Trash?	Sorting Opinion Writing	Individual	52
Where's Wendy?	Prepositions	Individual	53
What's for Dinner?	Adjectives/Plural Nouns	Individual	54
Eek! It's a Mouse!	Descriptive Writing	Individual	55
Me First!	Opinion Writing	Individual	56
This Is Me! 1	Informative Writing Descriptive Details	Individual	57
This Is Me! 2	Informative Writing Descriptive Details	Individual	58
This Is Me! 3	Opinion Writing Descriptive Details	Individual	59
A Wrinkled Twinkle Rhyme	Spelling Patterns	Pair	60
Blue Plate Diner	Adjectives	Individual	61
Freaky Fruit	Descriptive Writing	Individual	62
Future Cars	Opinion Writing	Individual	63
Bird News	Descriptive Writing	Individual	64
Timeline	Narrative Writing	Individual	65
The Sinking Boat	Pronouns	Individual	66

Prompt	Language Link	Learning Setting	Page
Ask the Author	Interrogatives Informative Writing	Individual	142
AlphaZoo	Spelling Descriptive Details	Individual	143
Thumbs-up!	Spelling	Collaborative	144
Bam!	Punctuation Narrative Writing	Individual	145
Go Home!	Research	Pair	146
Life in Sunnyville	Suffixes	Pair	147
I Am Powerful!	Suffixes	Individual	147
Wink, Blink, and Nod	Spelling Verbs	Collaborative	148
On the Road-e-o	Spelling Patterns	Pair	149
What's for Lunch, Duck?	Opinion Writing	Individual	150
Letter Soup Level 1	Spelling	Collaborative	151
Letter Soup Level 2	Spelling	Collaborative	151
Operation I	Spelling Patterns	Individual	152
Operation II	Spelling Patterns	Pair	152
Hank's Wish	Narrative Writing	Individual	153
Whoo Are Your Friends?	Verbs	Individual	154
The Sky Is Falling!	Narrative Writing Descriptive Details	Individual	155
The Bear or the Bee	Opinion Writing	Individual	156
The Talking Toy Box	Complete Sentences	Individual	157
Would You Ever?	Opinion Writing	Individual	158
Mood Ring	Opinion Writing	Individual	159
What Did You See at the Sea?	Verbs	Individual	160
Shh! Don't Wake Buddy!	Narrative Writing	Individual	161
Little Sister	Informative Writing	Individual	162
Hop on Board!	Narrative Writing	Individual	163
Energy Drink	Informative Writing	Individual	164
Whose Hat Is That?	Opinion Writing	Individual	165
Farmer Jones	Spelling	Individual	166
Farmer Jones Rides Again	Sentences	Individual	166

Chapter Three:
Mini-lessons and Sample Prompts

Learning to write is a process; it's a step-by-step process. Students will go through the steps for mastery as they learn how to become writers. Teachers will teach and model the concept, providing guided practice, until students are able to implement the skills independently. When modeling, it is critical that students see teachers go through the thought processes that include writing's struggles, frustrations, and rewards. Sometimes, prepared samples leap over these processes. It works particularly well when thinking is done visually—writing, marking out, rethinking—until a solution is achieved. I have personally seen more lightbulbs come on when I work through a problem, such as writing a claim or thesis statement, pairing my actions with teacher talk (more commonly known as talking to one's self). But it works. Often if we make something look too effortless, it can increase students' own anxiety about not being able to toss a well-developed idea onto paper the first time around. It just doesn't happen that way—at least not for me—and students need to know this. It underscores the idea that writing is indeed a learned craft and not an inherited trait.

Many of the prompts in *Take 5!* provide opportunities for practicing informative and opinion writing, two key focus areas in today's educational standards. While the prompts themselves require only brief exposure to the writing process, the lesson extensions can be used to develop students' quick writes into more developed essays. So how can this be accomplished?

The three mini-lessons provided here can help students visualize the writing process, discover purpose in writing, and develop a hook (students can't begin working on this early enough). Teachers can use these at the appropriate point in their students' writing journey. Some teachers may want to begin with these at the beginning of the year to initiate this yearlong writing adventure.

Mini-lesson 1:
Extended Analogy for the Writing Process

Often, it is a teacher's challenge to find a way to move students from the idea phase to the finished written product. One way to do that is by the use of a common analogy. In this case, the idea of going fishing is used to model the writing.

Modeling the Task: The "Write" Way to Fish

Mr. Brooks walked into Room 14. Something was strange. He wore a fishing hat and rubber boots.

"Good morning, class," his voice boomed. "Are you ready for a little fishing?"

"Fishing?" his class cried out.

"Fishing," he said again. "But first, we need the right tools."

Kelly frowned. "But Mr. Brooks, I thought we were writing, not fishing."

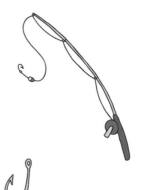

"Let's take a look at both," he said. "Fishing and writing are a lot alike. They need the right tools and a little work. Let's compare them."

1. **BAIT**
   "The bait I use for fishing is a worm. The bait I use for writing is an interesting idea, or a **hook**. A writing hook grabs the reader's attention."

2. **FISHING POLE**
   "The pole holds the line, the hook, the bait, and (maybe) the fish. It is the **main** tool for fishing. You can't fish without a pole. You can't write without a **main, or big, idea**. It would be like tossing worms into a lake or words onto a page."

3. **HOOK**
   "The hook catches the fish. A hook can also catch grass, a boot, or an old net. But you only want a fish, so toss everything else aside.

Writers hook many ideas. Some **support** the main idea; some do not. So we toss those back and hook another idea."

4. **TACKLE BOX**

"A tackle box **sorts** all the things you need for fishing. There's a place for extra hooks and a place for lures like plastic worms. There is even a place for small lead weights. These carry the hook and bait down to the fish. A writer also needs a tool for sorting ideas like an idea map or other organizers to put like ideas together. This keeps your tackle box, and your writer, more **organized**."

5. **PAIL**

"Catch a fish? Put it in a pail. The pail holds the fish. Writers also need a pail for their ideas. This pail is called a **paragraph** or **essay**. It holds all the ideas together."

Mr. Brooks finished. "And that's how we fish—um—I mean, write."

Practicing the Activity

Now it's your turn. With a partner, think of another way to explain the writing process. For example, compare it to taking a trip or cooking a meal or starting the first day of school.

Mini-lesson 2:
A Story's Purpose: Following a Road Map for Writing

Will we write a funny story? Will we write about a pet? We need a writing purpose. A purpose is like a road map. It leads the writing along. Writing can go in four major directions.

Modeling the Task

Purpose 1: Description (What it looks like)—A Day at the Zoo

Today, we went to the zoo! What did we see? We saw a large lion. We saw leafy green trees. What else did we see, hear, and smell at the zoo? Let's describe the zoo. Monkeys swung from vine to vine. A tall giraffe slowly munched on leaves. Colorful birds sang in the trees.

Purpose 2: Information (What we know)—The Science Museum

Today, we went to the science museum. They gave us much information. They told (informed) us about plants and trees. A tree is a tall plant made of wood. Plants help keep our air clean. Some plants can eat insects!

Purpose 3: Storytelling or Narrative (What happened)— The Boat Ride

Today, we went to the beach. We lay down on a blanket and quickly fell asleep. Soon, I dreamed of a bright, sunny day. I was on a boat. Then a dark cloud appeared. The water became very rough. A huge wave crashed over the boat. Oh no! What happened next? I grabbed two life jackets and threw one to my friend. The boat was sinking, so we jumped in the water. Suddenly, I woke up soaking wet! What a dream!

Purpose 4: Opinion (What I think)—Who Wants Pizza?

Need a new book or toy? Want pizza for dinner? Let's not fuss or argue about it. Just give a good reason. We will listen. We are open to all opinions. What you think and believe is your **opinion**. An opinion needs good reasons for support.

"Let's order pizza for dinner."
"Why?"
"Because I like it."

Is that a good reason? No. Other members of the family might not like pizza. Let's try a better reason.

"Let's order pizza because …

- *Everyone can choose a favorite topping.*
- *It doesn't cost much. You can buy two for the price of one.*
- *Traffic is bad. It can be delivered.*
- *It can take a long time to make something in the kitchen. This gives more time for homework and other stuff."*

With these reasons, you just might get that pizza tonight!

Practicing the Activity

Bedtime for Bailey (opinion writing)

It's 8:00. Time for bed.

"Not now," Bailey begs. "Please! Just a few more minutes."

"Why?"

"Because …."

Write or draw two reasons.

Achoo! (opinion writing)

Bailey has a cold. She coughs all day. Her nose is running.

"Stay away from me, Bailey!" her friend says.

"Give me two good reasons," Bailey hacks.

OK, we will. With a partner, write or draw two good reasons from Bailey's friend. Use the words *because, also,* or *and* in your answer. Let's keep her far, far away.

Mini-lesson 3:
A Writing "Hook":
Four Attention-getting Hooks

Many stories begin with these words:

"Once upon a time long, long ago … " OR "It was a dark and stormy night …."

These are called **hooks**. You can hang clothes on a hook. Fish bite a hook. Curtains hang on a hook. Hooks hold things. A story hook will hold a reader's attention. A good hook will hold readers' attention for a long time. They will want more of the story. Why? Because they've been hooked! Here are four types of hooks for writing.

Hook 1: An imagined event

> *No one really saw him. He was just there, just a little worm. Then slowly he removed his dull, dusty coat. All eyes lit up!*

What will come next? Readers will read about caterpillars' colorful change into butterflies in this **informative** story.

Hook 2: Unusual words and phrases

> *Lick, slurp, yum, crunch! It was one of the best vacations ever.*

The writer will then describe this vacation. This will be **descriptive** writing.

Hook 3: Someone's words

> *"Everyone stay on the bus!" the teacher yelled. "Just remain calm."*

The writer has a funny story about a class field trip. The story seems very serious at first. What could have happened? This writing is storytelling, or **narrative** writing.

Hook 4: Question

"Do we have to eat turkey on Thanksgiving?"

This writer has a different opinion. She would like hamburgers on Thanksgiving. This story will be **opinion** writing. The writer will give reasons for supporting her idea.

With a partner, write four hooks. Above the hook, write the purpose of the story. Grab the audience's interest!

Hook	Modeling the Task	Practicing the Activity
Imagined Event	**All About Bears** *Slowly, they entered the cave. It looked empty. Was that a growl?* *"Let's get out of here!"* This story will give facts about bears (informative writing). Now try creating a similar hook.	**Honeybees** Writing purpose: This story will explain how bees make honey (**informative writing**). Create an imagined event to hook the audience.
Unusual Words and Phrases	**Pet Store** *"Meow! Woof! Hiss! Everyone does NOT need a pet."* You have an opinion on pets. This story gives your reasons. Now try creating a similar hook.	**Recycling** Writing purpose: This story will give an opinion on recycling and trash (**opinion writing**). Write a hook for this article using unusual words or phrases.

Hook	Modeling the Task	Practicing the Activity
Someone's Words/ Dialogue	**Christopher Columbus** *"Are we there yet, Christopher Columbus?"* These words, spoken as a question, will begin a fiction story about a person on the boat with Christopher Columbus. Now try creating a similar hook.	**The Lost Elf** Writing purpose: Write a hook for a story about an elf. He became lost in a big storm (**narrative writing**). How will this story begin?
Asking a Question	**A Strange Breakfast** *"Would you eat green eggs?"* This describes a very strange breakfast on your vacation. Now try creating a similar hook.	**Saturday Morning** Writing purpose: This writing will describe the sights, sounds, and smells of a lazy Saturday morning in and around your home (**descriptive writing**). How will it begin?

And now we are ready to Take

4

Chapter Four:
The Prompts

What's the Big Idea?

Boom! Crash! This is a big storm! The roads are filled with water. It is very dark outside. The lights have gone out! The wind is blowing hard. Thunder and flashes of light fill the night air. What's the big idea?

Storms can be dangerous.

The big idea is supported with details.

Draw a circle on your paper. Draw four arrows. Point them at the circle. Read this paragraph:

The rain has stopped. The sun is shining again. Tree leaves and bushes look fresh and clean. People are coming outside. Some are walking their dogs. People are smiling and laughing. What's the big idea?

In the large circle, write a new big idea. Use only four or five words. On each arrow, write supporting details for your big idea. Use only five to six words for each one. All details will point to the big idea.

Ready? Take

LANGUAGE LINK
Informative Writing

LEARNING SETTING
Individual

DEPTH OF KNOWLEDGE

SUPPLIES
Journal, pencil

STANDARD
I can provide supporting details for a topic in informative writing.

LET'S EXPLORE MORE
Martha the Little Mouse by Janey Louise Jones. Superfairies. North Mankato, MN: Capstone, 2016. (K–3)

LANGUAGE LINK
Spelling Patterns
Opinion Writing

LEARNING SETTING
Individual

DEPTH OF KNOWLEDGE

SUPPLIES
Journal, pencil

STANDARDS

I can spell words by using spelling patterns.

I can support my opinion with reasons.

LET'S EXPLORE MORE

Dinnertime in the Forest:
Students can create their own food-friendly prompts. They simply choose an animal and create a fill-in-the-blank puzzle as in "Leap Frog" with possible food choices (e.g., squirrel and nut). They can then share with their classmates to solve.

Frankly, I Never Wanted to Kiss Anybody!: The Story of the Frog Prince as Told by the Frog by Nancy Loewen. The Other Side of the Story. North Mankato, MN: Capstone, 2014. (2–3)

Watch and listen to "The Vowel Song" by Elearnin on YouTube.

Leap Frog

The frog leaps across the pond. It is looking for food. Something is missing. Write the missing letter. Help feed the frog.

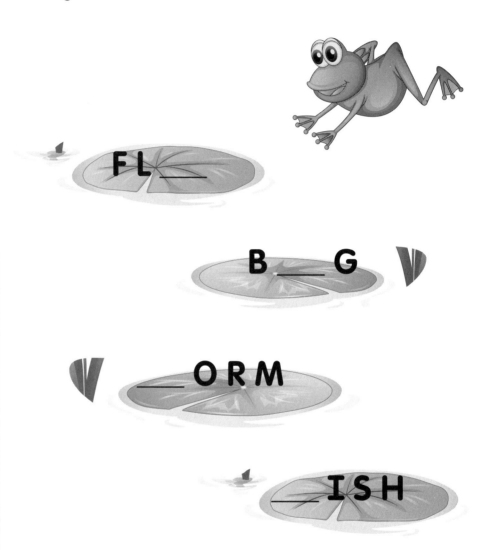

Complete this sentence.

I would/would not (circle one) like to be a frog because

_____.

Ready? Take 5!

Pete the Pelican

One early morning, Pete the brown Pelican swoops across the water. A flash of light catches his eye. Down he dives and up his rises with a fish in his bill. That is a nice catch, Pete! Color the picture of Pete. Glue or staple the picture to a page in your journal. Leave room at the bottom of the page. Under the picture, make a list numbered 1 to 3. What else will Pete do today? Begin each line with an action verb, and underline each verb.

Here is an example:

1. <u>Watch</u> a whale <u>wave</u> his tail.

Ready? Take

LANGUAGE LINK

Verbs

LEARNING SETTING

Individual

DEPTH OF KNOWLEDGE

● ● ○ ○

SUPPLIES

A coloring page of a pelican available on the Internet, glue, journal

STANDARD

I can use verbs.

LET'S EXPLORE MORE

Students will enjoy seeing photographs of pelicans, some with close-ups of their hooked bills and large pouches. Photos can be viewed on National Geographic's website by searching for "pelican." Some photos offer close-ups of a pelican catching its prey, like Pete!

Pet Names

My dog's name is Salty Pepper. What is your dog's name?

My cat's name is Tinky Pinky. What is your cat's name?

Names begin with a very big letter. Let's write silly names. Use little letters after the big letter.

Puppy dog, puppy dog, what is your name?

B_____   P_____

Kitty cat, kitty cat, what is your name?

M_____   K_____

Bunny rabbit, bunny rabbit, what is your name?

C_____   D_____

Little lamb, little lamb, what is your name?

G_____   L_____

And my name is

_____   _____

Ready? Take **5!**

True or False

On Monday, Ms. Green's class sat in a circle. Today was story time. Raphael stood first.

Raphael talked about his grandfather's goat farm. This summer Raphael stayed with his grandparents. He helped feed the goats and clean the barn. They turned the goats' milk into ice cream.

Logan stood up next. He talked about the tiny Quirts. Quirts live throughout the Black Forest. The King of the Quirts rides a large white rat. He also has magical powers. The other Quirts are afraid him. He can turn them into flies.

Fiction is about imaginary stories and people. Logan's story was fiction. Raphael's story was nonfiction. It was about real people or events. *Non* means *not*. *Non + fiction = not fiction*, or *nonfiction*.

You try it! Here is the topic: cats. First, write two facts about cats. This will be nonfiction. Then, write two sentences for a fiction story about cats. Include at least two words with prefixes, using the words below. Then share your writing with the class.

prefix	word	meaning
dis	disagree	not agree
im	impossible	not possible
in	incorrect	not correct
un	unafraid	not afraid

Ready? Take 5!

LANGUAGE LINK

Prefixes

LEARNING SETTING

Individual

DEPTH OF KNOWLEDGE

SUPPLIES

Journal, pencil

STANDARD

I can use prefixes and/or suffixes to figure out word meanings.

LET'S EXPLORE MORE

Listen to the song "Prefix or Suffix?" by The Bazillions on YouTube.

LANGUAGE LINK
Sorting

LEARNING SETTING
Individual

DEPTH OF KNOWLEDGE

● ◐ ◐ ◐

SUPPLIES

Journal, colored pencils

STANDARD

I can sort common words or objects into categories.

LET'S EXPLORE MORE

Rain, Rain, Go Away by Steven Anderson. Tangled Toons. North Mankato, MN: Cantata Learning, 2016. (1–3)

The Wizard of Oz Colors by Jill Kalz. The Wizard of Oz. North Mankato, MN: Capstone, 2014. (1–2)

The Colors of the Rainbow

See that rainbow in the sky? See the bands of color? Rainbows have different colors. One color is red. I see the color red on an apple. Another color is orange. Orange is the color of a carrot.

On each band, write down objects that may be the same color (like yo-yo for yellow). Next, lightly color each band.

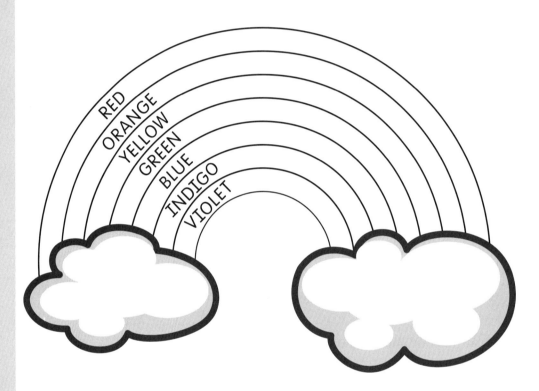

Ready? Take 5!

Duck!

One fall morning, a flock of ducks flew high overhead. They were heading south for the winter. Below them a clear pond came into view. It's time to eat! Down they dove! Yum! These were hungry ducks! They ate small insects and plants. Uh-oh! Next year, the pond may not be there. Someone wants to build a house there. Another person wants to keep the pond. Think deeply about this problem. Write one reason to help save the pond. Next, write one reason to support building the house. Include the word "because" or "then" in your answer.

I think _____

because/then _____

_____.

....

Ready? Take

SUPPLIES

Assortment of picture books (one for each pair), journal, pencil

STANDARD

I can describe people, places, things, and events with relevant details.

LET'S EXPLORE MORE

Picture This: This activity can be repeated as a whole class activity. After displaying a photograph, illustration, or painting for the class, have students record in their journal two specific objects—the object seen first and the object seen second. Students will then provide descriptive details beside each object. An informal class survey may be taken on their favorite object. What made this object stand out from all the rest? Discuss perspective in art and in writing.

Do You See What I See?

Let's look at our book. It has many colorful pictures. Choose one picture from the book. Look at it closely. What do you each see? Don't share your thoughts yet! Complete each sentence in your journal. (No peeking!)

I first see a _____.

It is/has _____.

Next, I see a _____.

It is/has _____.

Finished? Now, trade journals with your partner. Discuss these questions together:

- Did you see the same objects?

- No? What was different?

- Yes? Did you describe them in the same way?

- Were they in the same order? Why?

Ready? Take

Let's Go!

The sun is shining. It's warm outside. What will we do?

Will we fly **over** the **moon**?

Will we climb **up** a **hill**?

Will we skate **across** a **lake**?

Will we ride **on** an **alligator**?

Copy the list below and fill in the blanks. Write a preposition in the first blank. Write a noun in the second blank.

1. First, we ran _____ a _____.
           (preposition)   (noun)

2. Next, we jumped _____ a _____.
           (preposition)   (noun)

3. Then, we fell _____ a _____.
           (preposition)   (noun)

4. Last, we fell _____ a _____.
           (preposition)   (noun)

Ready? Take **5!**

LANGUAGE LINKS
Prepositions
Nouns

LEARNING SETTING
Individual

DEPTH OF KNOWLEDGE

SUPPLIES
Journal, pencil

STANDARDS
I can use many different prepositions (position words).

I can notice frequently occurring nouns and verbs.

LET'S EXPLORE MORE
Draw a map of the events enjoyed during your day! Place the correct number by each event.

What Is a Preposition? by Sheri Doyle. Parts of Speech. North Mankato, MN: Capstone, 2013. (K–1)

"Where Is the Mouse?" Do an Internet search for "Angles365 cat mouse game" to find this preposition game.

What's New at the Zoo?

It's field trip day! We are going to the zoo. Look at all the animals. I see lions and tigers. I see monkeys and bears. Wait! What is that strange animal? What does it look like? Fill in the blanks with words or pictures.

Its head is as round as a beach ball. _____.

Its tail is as long as a/an _____.

Its legs are as thin as _____.

Its teeth are as sharp as _____.

Its eyes are as big as _____.

Its fur is as red as _____.

Write a name for this animal _____.

Next, draw this very strange animal.

Ready? Take **5!**

Color Squares

Choose a color square. Tape it into your journal. Think about it. What is the same color as your square? It could be the ocean, a flower, a rock, and so on. Under the color square, list objects of this color. Need help? Look at picture books for more ideas. Finished? Select another color square and repeat the activity.

Ready? Take

LANGUAGE LINK
Capitalization

LEARNING SETTING
Individual

DEPTH OF KNOWLEDGE

SUPPLIES

Journal, pencil

STANDARD

I can capitalize words.

LET'S EXPLORE MORE

The "Capital" Game: Play the "Capital" game with the whole class. On a screen, show a series of words (or use large, handwritten cards). Some words use the capital letter correctly; some do not. If it's correct, the class calls out "correct"; if incorrect, the class calls out "incorrect." Examples: *the sun rose high into the sky* (incorrect); *Allie* (correct); *toe* (correct); *florida* (incorrect); *monday* (incorrect). Use a variety of names, places, and dates. Take a moment to review each word, explaining why it is or isn't correct.

Poppy's Puppy by Michele Jakubowski. Perfectly Poppy. North Mankato, MN: Capstone, 2015. (K–2)

Search for "Write Uppercase Letters" on the Turtle Diary website. Use this interactive activity to practice writing capital letters. Just follow the dots! The ABC Writing Chart on page 189 could be used with this activity.

Lucy's Puppies

Look! Your dog Lucy is a new mother. Look at all the puppies! One, two, three, four puppies! Draw four puppies in your journal. Write a name above each puppy. Make the first letter of each name a capital letter. Under the picture, write the color of each puppy. Is it brown, white, tan, gold, or black? Maybe it has two colors. Do not use capital letters for the colors.

Next, write a message to a friend. Tell your friend the big news! Write all names in capital letters. Be sure to capitalize the first word in each sentence. Circle each capital letter.

Ready? Take **5!**

The Birthday Box

1-2-3! Surprise! It's your birthday party. Look at that big box! Quick! Tear off the paper. Open it up! It's a box of Bs! I see a brand new baseball, a big book, bubble bath, and a beach ball. What else is inside? Write a list of words. They must begin with "B."

....

Ready? Take

DEPTH OF KNOWLEDGE

● ○ ○ ○

SUPPLIES

Journal, pencil

STANDARD

I can spell simple words by sounding them out.

LET'S EXPLORE MORE

Another Birthday Box: The birthday party can continue! On another day, a different letter can be wrapped inside the box. Students can select the letter of the day and work in pairs.

Scooby-Doo's Color Mystery by Benjamin Bird. Scooby-Doo! North Mankato, MN: Capstone, 2015. (PreK–K)

SUPPLIES

Journal, colored pencils, "Xplain" Your Writing Graphic Organizer (p. 184)

STANDARD

I can write narrative events in the correct order.

LET'S EXPLORE MORE

A Mouthful of Onomatopoeia by Bette Blaisdell. Words I Know. North Mankato, MN: Capstone, 2014. (1–2)

Whoosh, Crunch, Roar: Football Onomatopoeia by Mark Weakland. Football Words. North Mankato, MN: Capstone, 2016. (2–4)

Splat, Rip, and Roar

A balloon **pops**! The dog **growls**. A duck **quacks.** *Pop, growl,* and *quack* are sound words. Sound words are all around us. Here are more sound words:

ring	drip	purr
clap	moo	honk
splash	crash	roar
splat	crunch	buzz

Let's write a story with sounds only. Use words from the list or create your own. Using your "Xplain" sheet, begin the story in plain 1 and end in plain 4. Use one or more sound words in each plain. On the back of your paper, explain this story using words or pictures.

Ready? Take

Kings Bree and McFee

Once there were two brothers. King Bree was a very serious leader. In another castle far away, his brother, King McFee, was very silly. *Serious* means the opposite of *silly*. These words are antonyms. They are opposites like *cold* and *hot*. Here are more opposite word pairs.

bad/good	high/low
add/subtract	first/last
big/little	long/short
clean/dirty	top/bottom
open/close	right/wrong
cold/hot	stop/go
bright/dark	win/lose
happy/sad	wet/dry

Select two word pairs. Write two sentences for each pair. The first sentence will use the first word. The second sentence will use the second word, its antonym. Maybe you can use the brothers in your sentences!

Ready? Take

Letter Swap

Bart has a new game. It is called "Letter Swap." He touches a button on the game screen. A four-letter word appears. He swaps one letter in the word for a different letter. A new word appears. He swaps another letter. A different word appears. The goal is to make many new words.

The game goes like this:

Bart touches a button. The word *ring* appears.

Bart changes the letter *r* to *s.* The new word is now *sing.*

This time, Bart changes the letter *g* for *k.* The word is now *sink.*

Are you following the game? Each time Bart changes a letter, a new word appears.

Bart next changes the letter *i* for *a.* The word becomes *sank.*

He changes the letter *s* for *t.* The word *tank* appears.

Now it's your turn. Write these words across the top of your page:

> boy   sad   tap

Cross out one letter in each word. Change it to another letter. Write the new word under the first word. Continue changing letters and making new words. How far can you go?

Ready? Take

The Very Verby Vacation

Ricky is so excited! He is going to the beach. He has planned the best trip ever. Look at his list. The first word is an action verb.

Build a sand castle

Surf a big wave

Pick up seashells

Swim in the ocean

Fly a kite

Sorry, Ricky! None of these things happened. It rained all week! It was the worst trip ever! What did Ricky really do? Make a new list. Number your paper from 1 to 5. Begin each item with an action verb. These verbs will show a different time, or tense. He did these things in the past. You will need past tense verbs. Examples: Ricky *sorted* his socks. Ricky *cut* his toenails.

Ready? Take **5!**

LANGUAGE LINK
Verbs

LEARNING SETTING
Individual

DEPTH OF KNOWLEDGE

SUPPLIES
Journal, pencil

STANDARD
I can use the past tense of common verbs.

LET'S EXPLORE MORE
"What Did You Do Today?" by ELF Learning allows students to repeat the past tense in this series of videos available on the Internet.

Beach Bummer by Michele Jakubowski. Perfectly Poppy. North Mankato, MN: Capstone, 2014. (K–2)

SUPPLIES

Two slips of paper per student, pencils, cup, journal

STANDARD

I can determine the meaning of a compound word by using the two individual words.

LET'S EXPLORE MORE

Thumbtacks, Earwax, Lipstick, Dipstick: What Is a Compound Word? by Brian P. Cleary. Minneapolis, MN: Millbrook Press, 2013. (2–3)

Bottleplants and Eggtrees

A *birdhouse* is a house for birds. A *bedroom* is a room with a bed. *Birdhouse* and *bedroom* are compound words. They are made of two other words. Let's have some fun!

Get with your group. Take two slips of paper. Each person will write one noun on each slip. Toss both pieces of paper into the cup. Shake it well! Each person draws two slips of paper. Put the two words together. In your journal, write your new word (any order). Beside the word, write a definition. It's OK to be silly! Next, let each person in the group share the word and definition. Example: *bottleplant*—a plant that grows bottles!

Ready? Take 5!

A Peachy Preposition

Yum! A peach tree grows **in** Estela's backyard. Ripe peaches hang **from** the tree limbs. Estella takes a basket **to** the tree. She picks two peaches and puts them **into** the basket. Watch out! A squirrel has run **up** the tree. He grabs a peach. He then runs **down** the tree. Estella chases **after** him.

Follow that squirrel! What happens next? Where does he go? Write three more sentences. Use a preposition in each sentence. Write each preposition in red. End the story with one last sentence. Does the squirrel or Estella get the peach?

Ready? Take

LANGUAGE LINK
Prepositions Narrative Writing

LEARNING SETTING
Individual

DEPTH OF KNOWLEDGE
● ○ ○ ○

SUPPLIES
Journal, pencil, red colored pencil

STANDARDS
I can use prepositions (position words).

I can write narrative events in the correct order.

LET'S EXPLORE MORE

Watch Out, Nate!: On another day, use this same narrative prompt idea with Nate, a skateboard whiz. In pairs, students will write the narrative using prepositions. Where did Nate go? What happened at the end?

Squirrels by Mari Schuh. Backyard Animals. North Mankato, MN: Capstone, 2015. (K–1)

What Is a Preposition? by Sheri Doyle. Parts of Speech. North Mankato, MN: Capstone, 2013. (K–1)

SUPPLIES
Journal, pencil

STANDARD
I can understand and use question words (interrogatives).

LET'S EXPLORE MORE
The Rest of the Story: On another day, students can research the answers to their questions and share with the class or make a class book.

What's with the Long Naps, Bears? by Thomas Kingsley Troupe. The Garbage Gang's Super Science Questions. North Mankato, MN: Capstone, 2016. (K–2)

Bad News for Bears

You are a star reporter. Star reporters write good stories. A good story needs good questions and good answers.

Today, you are writing a story about bears. Black bears have been raiding trash cans during the night. Many people are scared of the bears. They want something done! You have four very good questions for your story. The first word is provided. You are to complete each question.

What _____?

How _____?

Why _____?

Where _____?

Ready? Take

Book Report

Erin likes to read a good book. Erin also likes sharing good books. Let's share one now! In your journal, finish these sentences.

This week I read _____.

It was written by _____.

The pictures were drawn by _____.

The best character was _____.

Circle one: I (liked/did not like) this book because

_____

_____

_____.

Now, draw your favorite part of the book.

LANGUAGE LINK
Opinion Writing

LEARNING SETTING
Individual

DEPTH OF KNOWLEDGE
● ● ○ ○

SUPPLIES
Journal, pencil

STANDARD
I can support my opinion with reasons.

LET'S EXPLORE MORE
Students can continue adding book report pages to their journals using other books they read.

Ready? Take **5!**

A Day at the Beach

It's a hot, sunny day. Let's go to the beach! Let's pack the car. What should we take? Select two of the most important items from the list. Write the name of the item by the number. Below the word, draw a picture of it and write one reason for packing the item. Which is the most important item to bring? Explain why.

umbrella   towel   blanket   beach ball   fishing pole

Follow the example.

1. food	2.	3.
Because we will be hungry.	Because	Because

Ready? Take **5!**

The Quiet Thief

In a land far, far away, there lived a **child** named Tomás. Tomás lived with his grandmother above her bakery. Every morning she rose early and began baking bread. The people of the village loved her bread! It smelled so good! But Tomás and his grandmother had a problem. Someone was stealing the bread.

One night, Tomás heard a sound downstairs. Was it a **person**? Was it a **wolf**? Slowly, Tomás crept down the stairs. He saw a **mouse**! It was sitting on a low **shelf**. The mouse was eating a **loaf** of bread. Quickly, Tomás stepped on the mouse's tail with his **foot**. He was a **hero**! He had caught the **thief**! But that was not the end of this tale. What happened the next night? Complete the story using the plural form for five of these words:

man – men	woman – women	wolf – wolves
shelf – shelves	loaf – loaves	foot – feet
hero – heroes	thief – thieves	child – children

Ready? Take **5!**

LANGUAGE LINK
Plural Nouns

LEARNING SETTING
Individual

DEPTH OF KNOWLEDGE
● ● ○ ○

SUPPLIES
Journal, pencil

STANDARD
I can use frequently occurring irregular plural nouns.

LET'S EXPLORE MORE
Mice Capades by Diana G. Gallagher. Pet Friends Forever. North Mankato, MN: Capstone, 2015. (1–3)

Play the "Billionaire Noun Plurals Game" at the ESL Games World website.

LANGUAGE LINK
Plural Nouns

LEARNING SETTING
Individual

DEPTH OF KNOWLEDGE

SUPPLIES
Journal, pencil

STANDARD
I can form plural nouns by adding s or es to words.

LET'S EXPLORE MORE
Win a present for Roy in the "Singular or Plural? Game 1" at the Roy the Zebra website.

Fear in the Forest

In the blanks below, write the plural form of each word by adding *s* or *es*.

Three sly fox____ search the tall bush____. They are searching for food. Three bird____ see them. They fly over the tree____. They swoop across the grass____. "Beware; beware," their voice____ sing.

Two squirrel____ drop their stolen peach____ and run for safety. Three rabbit____ dive in a hole. Three bear____ hear the noise. They climb over rock____. They wade through stream____. Onward they charge with a loud roar! Then all is quiet. No sound____ can be heard. The scared hunter____ have run away.

Ready? Take 5!

Puppy Doctor

Poor puppy! He won't eat his food. He does not play with his toys. He seems so tired. Oh no! He must be sick. Pretend you are an animal doctor. What would you do? Write or draw three ways to help a sick puppy.

1. _____

2. _____

3. _____

Ready? Take

LANGUAGE LINK
Informative Writing

LEARNING SETTING
Individual

DEPTH OF KNOWLEDGE
● ● ○ ○

SUPPLIES
Journal, pencil

STANDARD
I can provide supporting details for a topic in informative writing.

LET'S EXPLORE MORE
Veterinarians Help by Dee Ready. Our Community Helpers. North Mankato, MN: Capstone, 2013. (K–1)

LANGUAGE LINK

Sorting
Opinion Writing

LEARNING SETTING
Individual

DEPTH OF KNOWLEDGE

SUPPLIES
Journal, pencil

STANDARDS
I can sort common words or objects into categories.

I can support my opinion with reasons.

LET'S EXPLORE MORE
What Can Live at the Beach? by John-Paul Wilkins. What Can Live There? Chicago, IL: Heinemann Library, 2015. (PreK–1)

Treasure or Trash?

Luis and Rey are headed to the beach. They are taking a large bucket with them. They are looking for sea treasures. Each treasure will be placed in the bucket.

At the beach, they walk slowly. They see lots of shells. They add them to the bucket. But that's not all! Hey! That does not belong on the beach. They toss it into the bucket. Quickly their bucket fills up. Look inside. These objects are in the bucket.

cup	balloon
shell	sand
sock	crab
feather	drinking straw
rope	sea grass

Make two lists in your journal. Label one list "treasures." Label the other list "trash." Write or draw each object in the correct list. At the bottom of the page, complete this sentence:

Trash does not belong on the beach because _____

_____.

Ready? Take

Where's Wendy?

It is a rainy day. Wendy and her brother cannot go outside.

"I know!" Wendy says. "Let's play hide-and-go-seek!"

Wendy hides first. Her brother looks and looks. He cannot find her, but she cannot hide from you! Draw Wendy hiding in two different places. Under each picture, write a sentence. Name her hiding place, and use one of these words (prepositions).

below	behind
beside	over
under	on
in	above
inside	by

Example:

Wendy is under the bed.

LANGUAGE LINK
Prepositions

LEARNING SETTING
Individual

DEPTH OF KNOWLEDGE

SUPPLIES
Journal, pencil

STANDARD
I can use prepositions (position words).

LET'S EXPLORE MORE
What Is a Preposition? by Sheri Doyle. Parts of Speech. North Mankato, MN: Capstone, 2013. (K–1)

Check out these musical preposition lessons on YouTube: "Preposition" by The Bazillions and "The Prepositions Song" by Scratch Garden.

What's for Dinner?

It's dinner time! We have had a long day. Let's call and order dinner. What do we want? Pizza, egg rolls, burgers, chicken, or hot dogs? It's your turn tonight. You choose!

You make a phone call. Someone answers.

"Hello, this is Food Palace. We have it all. Just place your order, please."

Place your order. Be very descriptive. For instance, a hot dog is a plain hot dog. Do you want ketchup or hot mustard on it? Onions or spicy chili? What will you order? Record the conversation in your journal. You may add many more items to your order.

"Hello, my name is _____.

First, I would like a/an _____
                                                      (adj.)

_____ with _____
      (noun)   (adj.)

_____ and _____
   (plural noun)   (adj.)

_____ ."
   (plural noun)

Draw a picture of your first order.

Eek! It's a Mouse!

"Eek!" Mother screamed. "A mouse is in the kitchen!"

"Are you sure?" her son asked.

"Yes!" she said. "It looked like this."

Fill in the blanks with the correct words. Use the word bank below for help.

It had a long, thin _____ and very small,

sharp _____. Also, it had two very

pointy _____. It was brown and

white in _____. On each side of

its nose were long, thin _____.

Its body was furry and _____.

round	color
ears	claws
tail	whiskers

Now, use the description and draw Mother's mouse.

LANGUAGE LINK
Descriptive Writing

LEARNING SETTING
Individual

DEPTH OF KNOWLEDGE

SUPPLIES
Journal, pencil

STANDARDS
I can describe people, places, things, and events with relevant details.

I can add drawings or details to a description to provide information.

LET'S EXPLORE MORE
The Missing Mouse by Jacqueline Jules. Sofia Martinez. North Mankato, MN: Capstone, 2015. (K–2)

There's a Mouse Hiding in This Book! by Benjamin Bird. Tom and Jerry. North Mankato, MN: Capstone, 2014. (PreK–2)

Visit the popular and interactive Tom & Jerry character page at the Capstone Kids website.

LANGUAGE LINK
Opinion Writing

LEARNING SETTING
Individual

DEPTH OF KNOWLEDGE

SUPPLIES
Journal, pencil

STANDARD
I can support my opinion with reasons.

LET'S EXPLORE MORE
You Can Write a Terrific Opinion Piece by Jennifer Fandel. You Can Write. North Mankato, MN: Capstone, 2013. (1–2)

Me First!

It's Saturday! Skeeter and his sister have big plans today. Skeeter loves the library. His sister Kesha loves the soccer field.

"Drop me off first," said Skeeter to his mother.

"No!" Kesha cried. "I must be first."

Complete these sentences.

Skeeter: We should go to the library first because

_____

_____

_____.

Kesha: That may be, but _____

_____

_____.

Who had the best argument? Why?

_____

_____

_____

Ready? Take 5!

This Is Me! 1

Let's learn more about you! Complete these sentences:

My name is _____.

I am _____ years old.

I enjoy _____ and _____.

I like reading about _____.

I have _____.

Next, complete the picture using the This Is Me! Body Template. Draw and color your hair. Draw your face. Draw a picture on your shirt. It could be a toy like a robot, ball, or doll. Next, draw a pair of jeans, shorts, a skirt, or other clothing. Draw your favorite shoes like flip-flops, boots, or tennis shoes.

....

Ready? Take

SUPPLIES

Journal, colored pencils, This Is Me! Body Template (p. 185)

STANDARDS

I can provide supporting details for a topic in informative writing.

I can add drawings or details to a description to provide information.

LET'S EXPLORE MORE

We All Do Something Well by Shelley Rotner. Shelley Rotner's World. North Mankato, MN: Capstone, 2013. (1–2)

We All Look Different by Melissa Higgins. Celebrating Differences. North Mankato, MN: Capstone, 2012. (K–1)

LANGUAGE LINK

Informative Writing
Descriptive Details

LEARNING SETTING

Individual Writing

DEPTH OF KNOWLEDGE

SUPPLIES

Journal, colored pencils, This Is Me! Body Template (p. 185)

STANDARDS

I can provide supporting details for a topic in informative writing.

I can add drawings or details to a description to provide information.

LET'S EXPLORE MORE

Jobs If You Like … (Series) by Charlotte Guillain. Chicago, IL: Heinemann Library, 2013. (1–3)

This Is Me! 2

Complete this sentence.

One day, I want to be a _____

so I can _____

_____

_____.

Next, draw this person at the bottom of the This Is Me! Body Template. Add the right clothes. Maybe it is a spacesuit or a baseball uniform or a chef's apron and tall hat. In the picture, add other objects. A zookeeper needs animals. A teacher needs students and a desk. A bridge builder needs a river or lake.

Ready? Take 5!

This Is Me! 3

Hey, friend! I have lots of friends, even you! A friend can live next door or far away. A friend can be a sister or brother. A friend can also be a teacher, your mom, or a coach. The postman can also be a friend. We can have so many friends! Who is one of your good friends? Complete this sentence:

_____

is a good friend because _____

_____

_____.

Next, draw this good friend using the This Is Me! Body Template. Add other objects to your picture. These objects will help describe this friend (like a baseball cap, ballet slippers, or desk).

Ready? Take

LANGUAGE LINK

Opinion Writing
Descriptive Details

LEARNING SETTING

Individual

DEPTH OF KNOWLEDGE

SUPPLIES

Journal, colored pencils, This Is Me! Body Template (p. 185)

STANDARDS

I can support my opinion with reasons.

I can add drawings or details to a description to provide information.

LET'S EXPLORE MORE

Should Charlotte Share?: Being a Good Friend by Rebecca Rissman. What Would You Do? Chicago, IL: Heinemann Library, 2013. (PreK–1)

LANGUAGE LINK
Spelling Patterns

LEARNING SETTING
Pair

DEPTH OF KNOWLEDGE

SUPPLIES
Journal, pencil

STANDARD
I can spell words by using spelling patterns.

LET'S EXPLORE MORE
Sing this familiar nursery rhyme with new lyrics.

Twinkle, Twinkle Little Star by Megan Borgert-Spaniol. Sing-Along Songs. North Mankato, MN: Cantata Learning, 2015. (1–3)

A Wrinkled Twinkle Rhyme

Here are two nursery rhymes. The one on the left we know well. The one on the right has many changes. The second poem appeared in the book *Alice's Adventures in Wonderland.* It isn't at all like the first poem!

Twinkle, Twinkle, Little Star	**Alice in Wonderland**
Twinkle, twinkle, little star,	Twinkle, twinkle, little bat,
How I wonder what you are,	How I wonder what you're at,
Up above the world so high,	Up above the world you fly,
Like a diamond in the sky.	Like a tea tray in the sky.

Now it's your turn. With a partner, change the words of this nursery rhyme.

(1) Twinkle, twinkle, little _____,

(2) How I wonder _____,

(3) Up above the world _____,

(4) Like a _____ in the _____.

Repeat lines one and two.

Ready? Take **5!**

Blue Plate Diner

Everyone loves the Blue Plate Diner. Tonight, Karla and Kaelyn will be eating there. Everything looks so good. Karla and Kaelyn are very different. They never order the same thing. What will they order? Write one or more describing words, or adjectives, before each item, or noun.

Example:

Karla: gooey peanut butter cookie

Kaelyn: crunchy oatmeal cookie

Karla:

_____ soup

_____ salad

_____ pizza

_____ pie

Kaelyn:

_____ soup

_____ salad

_____ pizza

_____ pie

Ready? Take

DEPTH OF KNOWLEDGE
● ○ ○ ○

SUPPLIES
Journal, pencil

STANDARD
I can use adjectives (describing words).

LET'S EXPLORE MORE
Describing Words: Adjectives, Adverbs, and Prepositions by Anita Ganeri. Getting to Grips with Grammar. Chicago, IL: Heinemann Library, 2012. (1–3)

What Is an Adjective? by Jennifer Fandel. Parts of Speech. North Mankato, MN: Capstone, 2013. (K–1)

Freaky Fruit

What a beautiful island! It has sandy beaches and waterfalls. It has tall trees and green plants. Look at all those fruit trees! I see pineapple plants and mango trees. I see coconut and banana trees. Wait a minute! What is that? I have never seen that fruit. It has a very odd shape, smell, and taste.

Describe it: _____

Looks like: _____

Smells like: _____

Tastes like: _____

Let's give it a name: _____

Draw this fruit and its tree.

Ready? Take 5!

Future Cars

What will cars in the future be like? Will they all be electric? Will they hover, or float, in the air? Will they fly from place to place? Will they have snack machines? What will they be?

Begin with a topic sentence: Cars of the future will be

very _____.

 (Example: fun, strange, quick, enjoyable)

Give two details to support your opinion.

1. _____

2. _____

End with a concluding sentence:

People will love these cars because _____

_____

_____.

Ready? Take

LANGUAGE LINK
Opinion Writing

LEARNING SETTING
Individual

DEPTH OF KNOWLEDGE
● ● ● ○

SUPPLIES
Journal, pencil

STANDARD
I can support my opinion with reasons.

LET'S EXPLORE MORE
Taking a Trip: Comparing Past and Present by Rebecca Rissman. Comparing Past and Present. Chicago, IL: Heinemann Library, 2014. (PreK–1)

"Create a Car": This activity on the ABCya website lets students design a car of the future—even with solar panels—that can be printed and attached to their journal entry.

Bird News

A bird flew into a nearby tree. No one had ever seen a bird like this. You have discovered a new bird. Now, you have an important job. You must write a description of it for the Nature World website. Remember, this is a very strange bird.

Name: _____

Description: _____

_____

Habitat (where they can be found): _____

Food: _____

Movements: _____

Add a picture to your description.

Ready? Take 5!

Timeline

Clark has done and seen many things. He remembers the time he:

Moved to a new town

Broke his leg in soccer

Learned to swim

Got lost on a hiking trip

What about you? Create a timeline of your life. Number from 1 to 5 in your journal. Write or draw five big, small, or even silly events in your life. Put them in the correct order.

Ready? Take

LANGUAGE LINK
Narrative Writing

LEARNING SETTING
Individual

DEPTH OF KNOWLEDGE

SUPPLIES
Journal, pencil

STANDARD
I can write narrative events in the correct order.

LET'S EXPLORE MORE
Timelines, Timelines, Timelines! by Kelly Boswell. Displaying Information. North Mankato, MN: Capstone, 2014. (1–2)

Students can practice thinking sequentially using the interactive timeline on the ReadWriteThink website.

LANGUAGE LINK
Pronouns

LEARNING SETTING
Individual

DEPTH OF KNOWLEDGE

SUPPLIES

Journal, pencil

STANDARD

I can use pronouns.

LET'S EXPLORE MORE

Captain Kidd's Crew Experiments with Sinking and Floating by Mark Weakland. North Mankato, MN: Capstone, 2012. (2–3)

What Is a Pronoun? by Sheri Doyle. Parts of Speech. North Mankato, MN: Capstone, 2013. (K–1)

The Sinking Boat

Oh no! Your boat is drifting away. You made a silly mistake. You did not tie it to the dock very well. It sank. Your dad will not be happy. Tell Dad your story. Use these words: *I, me, my, mine.*

"I _____

_____

_____

_____

_____."

Oh no! Your brother saw the whole thing. He likes bold tales of adventure. He will tell Dad a very different story of the sinking boat. Use these words: *he/she, him/she or her, his/hers.*

"He _____

_____

_____

_____

_____."

Ready? Take 5!

Match Game

Spread the word cards facedown across the table. Mix them around. The first person turns up two cards. Do the noun and verb match? No? Then turn them facedown again. The next player takes a turn. Matching cards are set to the side. The cards could look like this:

Card 1	Card 2
The boy	skate (no match)
The dog	skates (silly but matches)
Stars	winks (no match)

Continue until all cards are used.

Ready? Take

LEARNING SETTING
Collaborative

DEPTH OF KNOWLEDGE
● ● ◐ ○

SUPPLIES

Deck of premade word cards that include five singular verbs, five plural verbs, five singular nouns, and five plural nouns (one deck for each group of students). These can be made from construction paper, or students can create their own decks on slips of paper.

STANDARD

I can use verbs and nouns that match tense.

LET'S EXPLORE MORE

Blast off into space at ipadthinker.com with the subject-verb agreement game.

LANGUAGE LINK
Narrative Writing

LEARNING SETTING
Pair

DEPTH OF KNOWLEDGE

SUPPLIES

Journal, pencil

STANDARD

I can write narrative events in the correct order.

LET'S EXPLORE MORE

Writing Stories (Series) by Anita Ganeri. Chicago, IL: Heinemann Library, 2014. (1–3)

The Pool Adventure

What can go wrong today? The sun is shining. The water in the pool looks so cool. You dive and swim around. Soon, you climb on a float and close your eyes. Splash! What happened?

Finish the story with a partner. Share with the rest of the class.

Ready? Take **5!**

Bus Stop

Cars, trucks, and buses travel over many different roadways. Highways go from city to city. A street might take you from your school to your house. Today, our bus will travel over different roadways. We will travel over a road, a lane, a drive, a place, a highway, an avenue, a court, a boulevard, a way, a terrace, a loop, or a circle.

In this group activity, one person is the bus driver. Everyone repeats the first line together: "Bus driver, bus driver, this is my stop." The bus driver then asks: "Where do you live?" The person on the right might say, "On Boom Boom Boulevard." Each player will select a word from the list. Try adding a word with the same letter before that word. It can be real or really silly!

Example:

All: "Bus driver, bus driver, this is my stop."

Bus driver: "Where do you live?"

First person: "On Licorice Loop."

Go all around the circle. Change bus drivers after each round.

....

Ready? Take

LANGUAGE LINK
Sorting

LEARNING SETTING
Individual

DEPTH OF KNOWLEDGE

SUPPLIES
Journal, pencil

STANDARD
I can sort common words or objects into categories.

LET'S EXPLORE MORE
Original Recipe by Jessica Young. Finley Flowers. North Mankato, MN: Capstone, 2016. (2–3)

Pizza Bar

Wow! What a pizza! It's called the Wild West Pizza. This pizza is loaded with onions, cheese, baked beans, chili, and barbecue chicken! Cowboys and cowgirls would love it! Create YOUR own pizza. Choose one of these pizza names or create one of your own.

Sweet Shop Pizza	Farmhouse Pizza
Day at the Beach Pizza	Cold Winter Day Pizza
Up in Space Pizza	Movie Night Pizza

Next, draw a large circle. Inside the circle, draw the toppings for your pizza. Make sure the toppings match the name of the pizza.

For example:

I will have an Underwater Pizza with crab and seaweed and fish sticks.

Ready? Take **5!**

Mr. Flip Flap

Mr. Flip Flap did not see the gum on the sidewalk. He stepped right on it! So he kept walking. First, he stepped on a paper bag. He didn't see it. So he kept walking. Flip flap.

Then, he stepped on a banana peel. He didn't see it. So he kept walking. Flip flap, flip flap.

Continue this story of Mr. Flip Flap. Use these transition words: *Next, After that, Soon, After a while, Also, At last.* Here is one example to use:

Next, he stepped on a/an _____.

After that, he stepped on a/an _____.

Soon, he _____.

After a while, he _____.

Also, he _____.

At last, he _____.

Ready? Take **5!**

LEARNING SETTING
Individual

DEPTH OF KNOWLEDGE

SUPPLIES

Journal, pencil

STANDARD

I can write narrative events in the correct order.

LET'S EXPLORE MORE

Students can make a word cloud of transitions on websites such as Wordle. Copies can be placed in journals for later reference.

What an Ending!

Question: What did she name her dog?

Answer 1: Lucky? (I'm not sure.)

Answer 2: Lucky. (This is the right answer.)

Answer 3: Lucky! (This is such a cool name!)

Look at these three answers. The same word was used three times. But there are three different answers. It's all a matter of punctuation. Now you try it. On your page, write this question: "Who is your new teacher?" Below it, answer the question three different ways.

It might look like this:

1. "Mr. Goolsby! (My brother had him. He said Mr. Goolsby was the best ever!)"

1. _____

2. _____

3. _____

Ready? Take **5!**

A Walk in the Park

Read the following story:

Brave Mr. Bland took a brisk walk one dark night. Quickly, he rushed through a dangerous park. Suddenly, he saw a very large dog. It was so huge! He quickly walked in the opposite direction. The dog was quite fast. Mr. Bland was so unhappy. He lost the dog. The dog was now his worst enemy.

Now, rewrite this same story with a partner. This time write a word that is opposite in meaning to the underlined word. For example, the opposite of "opposite" is the "same." Watch as a new story appears!

Ready? Take

LANGUAGE LINK

Antonyms

LEARNING SETTING

Pair

DEPTH OF KNOWLEDGE

● ● ○ ○

SUPPLIES

Journal, pencil

STANDARD

I can identify antonyms of words.

LET'S EXPLORE MORE

Eddie and Ellie's Opposites (Series) by Daniel Nunn. Chicago, IL: Heinemann Library, 2014. (PreK–K)

Words I Know (Series) by Bette Blaisdell. North Mankato, MN: Capstone, 2014. (1–2)

LANGUAGE LINK
Conjunctions

LEARNING SETTING
Individual

DEPTH OF KNOWLEDGE

SUPPLIES

Journal, pencil

STANDARD

I can use conjunctions
(connecting words).

LET'S EXPLORE MORE

Joining Words: Conjunctions by
Anita Ganeri. Getting to Grips
with Grammar. Chicago, IL:
Heinemann Library, 2012. (1–3)

What Is a Conjunction? by Jennifer
Fandel. Parts of Speech. North
Mankato, MN: Capstone, 2013. (K–1)

And Then What Happened?

The basketball game was over. Gordie and Scott began the long walk home. The sky was clear, **but** that soon changed. The wind began blowing, **and** it started raining. It seemed so dark, **yet** the moon shone brightly overhead. They began running, **so** they could escape the storm. They looked for a warm **and** dry place. Things seemed really scary, **yet** the worst was still to come.

What happened next? Continue this story. Use at least four different conjunctions: *for, and, but, or, so, yet, nor.*

Ready? Take

Aunty Ant

Two words can sound just alike, but they can have different meanings. An *ant* crawls on the ground. My *aunt* is my mother's sister. Read these two sentences:

That large *ant* is crawling on my *aunt.*

Wow! Humpty Dumpty *ate eight* doughnuts!

Now it's your turn! Select two word groups from the list below. Then write one sentence for each pair.

I/eye	night/knight	blue/blew
bare/bear	bury/berry	flower/flour
dear/deer	whole/hole	brake/break

Ready? Take

LANGUAGE LINK
Homonyms

LEARNING SETTING
Individual

DEPTH OF KNOWLEDGE
● ○ ○ ○

SUPPLIES

Journal, pencil

STANDARD

I can explain that some words have more than one meaning. (A *duck* is a **noun**; *to duck* is a **verb**.)

LET'S EXPLORE MORE

They're Up to Something in There: Understanding There, Their, and They're by Cari Meister. Language on the Loose. North Mankato, MN: Capstone, 2016. (2–4)

LANGUAGE LINK
Capitalization

LEARNING SETTING
Individual

DEPTH OF KNOWLEDGE

● ● ○ ○

SUPPLIES

Journal, pencil, copy of the map for each student

STANDARD

I can capitalize words.

LET'S EXPLORE MORE

Our School Campus: Students can take a walk around the school with journals in hand. Start with your classroom and walk around the campus. Students will draw the path. Back in class, they can give street names to each stretch of sidewalk. No sidewalk? Then they can use the word "road."

How to Read a Map by Melanie Waldron. Let's Get Mapping! Chicago, IL: Heinemann Library, 2013. (2–4)

Maps, Maps, Maps! by Kelly Boswell. Displaying Information. North Mankato, MN: Capstone, 2014. (1–2)

Hey, Taxi!

You are so excited. Tonight is the band concert. The concert starts at 6:00 p.m. You must be on time. Oh no! Your mom's car has broken down. Quick! Call a taxi. The taxi arrives, but the driver is new. Provide directions to the concert hall. Use the downtown map. Write names on each street. They may also be avenues or drives. Go both down and across. Capitalize each name. Next, draw the route for the taxi driver on the map.

Uh-oh! He is still confused. Under the drawing, write the directions carefully. How many blocks must he go? Does he turn right or left? Name each street.

You live here.

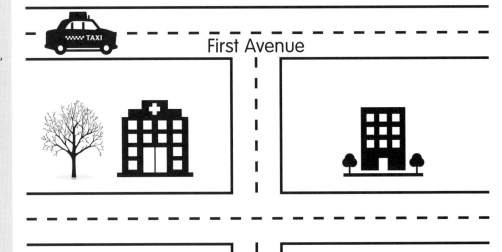

First Avenue

Concert Hall

Ready? Take

My Pet Obo

Let's make some Os. First, trace around things that are different-sized circles. Coins, the bottoms of cups, small cans, and other round objects in the classroom may be used. Use different colors of paper. You will need four to five circles. Next, cut out each circle. Be careful! Fold each circle in half. Start on one side of the fold and cut a semicircle to the other side. Reopen. You now have Os! On your paper, glue the Os so they overlap. Make one shape of overlapping Os. This is your pet Obo! Write three sentences about your pet. What kind of pet is it? What does it do? What does it eat? Does it have any powers? You must use the letter O in your sentences. How many Os can you use?

Ready? Take 5!

LANGUAGE LINK

Descriptive Writing

LEARNING SETTING

Individual

DEPTH OF KNOWLEDGE

● ● ● ○

SUPPLIES

Objects to trace various sizes of circles (pennies, bottle caps), scissors, colored construction paper, glue, journal

STANDARDS

I can describe people, places, things, and events with relevant details.

I can add drawings or details to a description to provide information.

LET'S EXPLORE MORE

Drawing Pets: A Step-By-Step Sketchbook by Mari Bolte. My First Sketchbook. North Mankato, MN: Capstone, 2015. (1–2)

Descriptive Writing

Individual

DEPTH OF KNOWLEDGE

SUPPLIES

Journal, colored pencils

STANDARDS

I can describe people, places, things, and events with relevant details.

I can add drawings or details to a description to provide information.

LET'S EXPLORE MORE

The Doggone Dog by Diana G. Gallagher. Pet Friends Forever. North Mankato, MN: Capstone, 2014. (1–3)

Reading Is Everywhere by Martha E. H. Rustad. Wonderful World of Reading. North Mankato, MN: Capstone, 2013. (K–1)

Lost Pooch

One day Brady saw a dog by the road. It had no collar. Its fur was tangled in knots. It seemed so lost and hungry. Brady picked up the little dog. He carried it to an animal shelter. Now we need your help. Create a sign. Begin with a title like "Dog Found." First, draw a picture of the dog. Next, add the following information:

He was found (where) _____.

He is (describe him) _____

_____.

Contact me at (address or phone number) _____

_____

_____.

This sign will be placed along roadways. It must be colorful and organized.

Ready? Take **5!**

A Bear+y Sad Story

One <u>cloudy</u>, <u>stormy</u> day, the <u>tallest</u> tree in the forest <u>topples</u> over. It <u>hits</u> a <u>buzzing</u> beehive.

A <u>sleepy</u> bear <u>slowly</u> <u>comes</u> out of his cave. He is <u>looking</u> for the noise. Pow! A bee <u>stings</u> him on his <u>stuffy</u> nose. Whack! Another bee <u>gets</u> into his <u>hairy</u> head. He <u>madly</u> <u>slaps</u> at it. He feels so <u>helpless</u>.

Help the poor bear. Finish his story and use word endings in your story. For example, here are some ways to change the word *cloud*:

Add a *y* to *cloud*. You get a *cloudy* day.

Add an *s* to *cloud*. You get many clouds, not one.

Add *less* to *cloud*. You get a clear sky with no clouds.

Here are more word endings: *s, er, est, ing, ly, y, less, ful.* This list will be very *help+ful*!

Ready? Take 5!

LEARNING SETTING
Individual

DEPTH OF KNOWLEDGE

SUPPLIES

Journal, pencil

STANDARD

I can use word endings (-ed, -es) and affixes (re-, un-, -ful, -less) to understand word meanings.

LET'S EXPLORE MORE

Look Inside a Bee Hive by Megan C. Peterson. Look Inside Animal Homes. North Mankato, MN: Capstone, 2012. (PreK–2)

LANGUAGE LINK
Compound Words

LEARNING SETTING
Individual

DEPTH OF KNOWLEDGE
● ○ ◐ ○

SUPPLIES
Journal, pencil

STANDARD
I can determine the meaning of a compound word by using the two individual words.

LET'S EXPLORE MORE

Daffy Definitions: Let's make compound words! Look around you. What do you see? List six words like *keys*, *pot*, or *light*. Now, combine these in different ways to make new words! Beside each word, write your definition. Example: plantkey. A keyplant is a plant that grows keys!

Sing along with the "Compound Boogie" song found on YouTube.

Word Bump

Bump! What was that noise? Two words just bumped into each other. It was a big bump! It made a whole new word. It is called a compound word. These are words like *football* and *skateboard*. A word bump looks like this.

dog ▶◀ **house**

A dog is an animal.
A house can be your home.
A doghouse is a home for dogs!

Let's bump some more words! Bump any of these nouns together. Beside the new word, write or draw the meaning. Words may be used more than once.

air	fish	moon
bed	flash	note
bird	friend	rain
boat	ham	room
book	hole	sail
bow	home	school
brow	house	ship
brush	lash	star
burger	life	tooth
day	lift	work
eye	light	worm

Ready? Take

Welcome Home!

Rafael is so happy! His mom is coming home. She is a member of the army. She has been far, far away from home. His friend Elena has an idea! She begins planning a "welcome back" parade! First, she writes letters to all the teachers.

Dear Teachers,

Rafael Perez is a good friend of mine. His <u>mom is</u> in the Army. <u>I am</u> asking for your help. <u>Let us</u> all stand on Second Avenue at 5:00 p.m. on Wednesday, January 2. <u>She will</u> arrive home then. <u>We will</u> all wear red, white, and blue. Bring your families and flags!

Thank you!
Elena Diaz

Now, it is time for the second part of her plan. She writes an invitation to Rafael's friends. She begins the letter:

Hey Good Buddies!

Rewrite Elena's first letter. Use apostrophes for the underlined words. Add or change words. <u>She'd</u> like your help. <u>It's</u> for a good cause!

Ready? Take

LANGUAGE LINK

Apostrophes
Formal vs. Informal Writing

LEARNING SETTING

Individual

DEPTH OF KNOWLEDGE

SUPPLIES

Journal, pencil

STANDARDS

I can use apostrophes in contractions.

I can compare formal and informal uses of English.

LET'S EXPLORE MORE

I Can Write Letters and E-Mails by Anita Ganeri. I Can Write. Chicago, IL: Heinemann Library, 2013. (1–3)

Special Forces by Ellen Labrecque. Heroic Jobs. Chicago, IL: Heinemann Library, 2012. (1–2)

U.S. Military Forces (Series) by Michael Green. North Mankato, MN: Capstone, 2013. (1–2)

LANGUAGE LINK
Narrative Writing

LEARNING SETTING
Collaborative

DEPTH OF KNOWLEDGE

SUPPLIES
Journal, pencil, space for groups to gather

STANDARD
I can write narrative events in the correct order.

LET'S EXPLORE MORE
A Cat Is Chasing Me Through This Book by Benjamin Bird. Tom and Jerry. North Mankato, MN: Capstone, 2015. (PreK–2)

Wiggle Worm, Wiggle Worm

Let's play "Wiggle Worm." Wiggle is always on the move. Everybody says: "Wiggle Worm, Wiggle Worm, what have you done?"

The first person will answer the question: "I met

_____, and we _____."

It might sound like this:
"I met a pirate and we found buried treasure."

Everybody repeats the first line again: "Wiggle Worm, Wiggle Worm, what have you done?" The next person then answers the question.

Here are some more ideas:
"I met a princess, and we rode off on a white horse." Or "I met a rabbit, and we hopped all over the house."

Go all around the circle. Later, in your journal, write or draw your favorite answer. Why was it your favorite?

Ready? Take **5!**

Help! Police!

After school, we come home, but it is very quiet. Oh no! Mirle, our dog, is missing! The police need a description of Mirle. Mom goes first. The policeman wrote down every word: "Mirle is a <u>large</u> dog. He has <u>snowy</u>, <u>curly</u> hair and very <u>wide</u> feet. He has <u>sharp</u> teeth, and his bark is a bit <u>powerful</u>. He is very <u>playful</u>. Also, he is very <u>friendly</u> and <u>loving</u>."

Now, it's your turn. Describe Mirle in your own words. Use a different word for each underlined word. The word, however, must be close in meaning to Mom's words. It might start like this: "Mirle is a <u>hefty</u> dog."

Ready? Take

LANGUAGE LINK

Synonyms
Adjectives

LEARNING SETTING

Individual

DEPTH OF KNOWLEDGE

● ● ○ ○

SUPPLIES

Journal, pencil

STANDARDS

I can use adjectives (describing words).

I can determine differences in meaning of similar verbs and adjectives.

LET'S EXPLORE MORE

Where's Mirle?: In groups, students can finish the narrative story of Mirle on another day. What happened to him? Did he ever make it back home? Compare the stories and examine the different perspectives with students. Stories can also be combined into a class book. Students in other classes can listen and then choose the best ending.

Thesaurus Rex by Michael Dahl. Library of Doom: The Final Chapters. North Mankato, MN: Capstone, 2016. (1–3)

What Is an Adjective? by Jennifer Fandel. Parts of Speech. North Mankato, MN: Capstone, 2013. (K–1)

Veggie Scramble

Look out! Someone bumped into a shelf. He knocked down the stacks of vegetables. Cans of beans, peas, corn, and beets are everywhere. You must stack them again. Draw FOUR stacks of vegetables. Count the cans carefully. The number of cans in your stacks should match the number of cans in the picture.

Now we have beans, peas, corn, and beets sorted. But we still have room on the shelf. We need another vegetable. What vegetable will you add? Why? Use the word *because* in your answer.

Ready? Take 5!

A Helpful Dinosaur

Sit. Stand. Stay. Fetch. Training a dog is hard. Training a dinosaur would be even harder. But maybe you could train a dinosaur to be very helpful. Maybe you can train it to light a campfire for delicious s'mores. Or maybe you can teach it to stretch across a pond. Then you can walk safely across. Perhaps your dinosaur can learn to get your kite from the top of a tree. But your dinosaur must be trained very carefully! Write a fun paragraph about training a dinosaur for a task. Begin with a topic sentence like this:

Training a dinosaur to _____

can be very _____.

Next, fill in each blank:

First, _____.

Next, _____.

Last of all, you _____.

Finally, provide one last important sentence for your paragraph. Try and make it a funny one.

Ready? Take *!*

LANGUAGE LINK
Narrative Writing

LEARNING SETTING
Individual

DEPTH OF KNOWLEDGE
● ● ○ ○

SUPPLIES
Journal, pencil

STANDARD
I can write narrative events in the correct order.

LET'S EXPLORE MORE
Dinosaurs: Can You Tell the Facts from the Fibs? by Kelly Liner Halls. Lie Detector. North Mankato, MN: Capstone, 2016. (K–3)

Show Me Dinosaurs: My First Picture Encyclopedia by Janet Riehecky. My First Picture Encyclopedias. North Mankato, MN: Capstone, 2013. (1–2)

LANGUAGE LINK
Narrative Writing

LEARNING SETTING
Individual

DEPTH OF KNOWLEDGE

SUPPLIES

Journal, pencil

STANDARD

I can write narrative events in the correct order.

LET'S EXPLORE MORE

Exploring Space (Series) by Martha E. H. Rustad. North Mankato, MN: Capstone, 2012. (K–1)

More days could be added to the journal at a later time after reading books or watching films on space travel.

Kid-in-Space

Five-four-three-two-one! Blast off! Look at you! You were selected for the Kid-in-Space Program. Now, you are flying through space. Two times a day you must report back to Earth. These are very brief reports of only two sentences each. It is day one. Finish the report.

Day One:

Today I _____

_____.

There was a problem with _____

_____.

Day Two:

Today I _____

_____.

I saw something really _____.

It _____

_____.

That's all for now!

Signed,

_____

Ready? Take **5!**

The Strange Bug

Objects look bigger under a magnifying glass or microscope. Examine the different objects with your magnifying glass. Let's be scientists today. You have found a very strange bug.

Draw a big circle on your page. This is your magnifying glass. Inside the circle, draw this bug. Does it have lots of legs? Is it long or short? Is it furry or smooth? Big or small? Does it have big eyes or tiny eyes? What colors do you see? Is it striped or spotted? Does it have horns? Draw your bug.

Under the drawing, give the bug a name. In a paragraph, answer these questions:

What does it look like?

How does it move?

Is it a helpful bug? How?

Does it sting?

Create other facts about your bug. Write one last sentence about your bug. Zap us with a great idea!

Ready? Take

LANGUAGE LINK
Descriptive Writing

LEARNING SETTING
Individual

DEPTH OF KNOWLEDGE
● ● ● ○

SUPPLIES
Journal, magnifying glasses (one for every 2–3 students), colored pencils

STANDARDS
I can describe people, places, things, and events with relevant details.

I can add drawings or details to a description to provide information.

LET'S EXPLORE MORE
Fingerprint Bugs by Bobbie Nuytten. Fun with Fingerprints. North Mankato, MN: Capstone, 2016. (K–1)

Yogi Bear's Guide to Bugs by Mark Weakland. Yogi Bear's Guide to the Great Outdoors. North Mankato, MN: Capstone, 2016. (1–2)

Letter Bingo

Let's play Bingo. This is how we play. Place all letter squares facedown. No letters can be seen. The first player turns over a letter square. The player must say a word that begins with this letter. Then the square is placed on the matching letter on the card. Can't think of a word? Then return the square with the other squares facing down. Play continues until all letters are covered.

Ready? Take 5!

The Very Busy Day

It's a busy day ahead! Your favorite cartoon, superhero, or movie character needs your help. Place the name at the top of the page. Next, list these times on your paper. Go down the page. Skip one line after each hour.

8:00 a.m.

9:00 a.m.

11:00 a.m.

1:00 p.m.

3:00 p.m.

5:00 p.m.

Organize the day for your character. What will he or she or it being doing at these times? Write a sentence beside the time. It might look like this:

1:00 p.m.—A reporter for *Comic Times* will take pictures.

Ready? Take

DEPTH OF KNOWLEDGE

● ● ○ ○

SUPPLIES

Journal, pencil

STANDARD

I can write narrative events in the correct order.

LET'S EXPLORE MORE

Toontastic app by Launchpad Toys, available from the iTunes App Store, allows students to create, animate, and record their own cartoons.

The Amazing Adventures of Superman! Battle of the Super Heroes! by Yale Stewart. DC Super Heroes. North Mankato, MN: Capstone, 2015. (K–2)

Timelines, Timelines, Timelines! by Kelly Boswell. Displaying Information. North Mankato, MN: Capstone, 2014. (1–2)

LANGUAGE LINK

Spelling
Capitalization

LEARNING SETTING

Individual

DEPTH OF KNOWLEDGE

● ○ ○ ○

SUPPLIES

Journal, pencil

STANDARD

With guidance and support from adults and peers, focus on a topic and strengthen writing as needed by revising and editing.

LET'S EXPLORE MORE

Punctuation: Commas, Periods, and Question Marks by Anita Ganeri. Punctuation. Chicago, IL: Heinemann Library, 2012. (1–3)

Macee's Big Mess

Macee's boss is not happy. Her news story is a mess! Her boss can't read the story. It needs help. Rewrite Macee's story. Correct her spelling and use capital letters. You may also use your own words as well. Her boss has underlined her mistakes.

Early <u>wensday</u> a <u>yonge</u> man in a <u>yelow</u> car drove <u>thru</u> a red <u>lite</u>. He <u>wuz</u> in a <u>grate</u> big <u>hurray</u>. He was going <u>too</u> the <u>liberry</u> for a safe <u>driveng</u> class. But he was going <u>to</u> fast! He hit a dump truck. <u>no</u> <u>won</u> was hurt.

Ready? Take 5!

Animal Tales

Animals can do some strange things like the animals in this short poem. The poem begins with a question word:

What kind of raccoon
Slurps from a spoon?
Or wraps colorful strings around the rings
Of his tail?

Notice the pattern in this poem. It has four lines.

The first line begins "What kind of _____"

The second line finishes the question and ends with a question mark.

The last words in line one and two rhyme.

The third line begins another question with "Or

_____"

The fourth line has only three words and finishes the question with a question mark.

Now it's your turn! Follow the pattern. With a partner, write a silly poem about another animal!

Ready? Take **5!**

LANGUAGE LINK

Interrogatives

LEARNING SETTING

Pair

DEPTH OF KNOWLEDGE

SUPPLIES

Journal, pencil

STANDARD

I can use question words.

LET'S EXPLORE MORE

Thorns, Horns, and Crescent Moons: Reading and Writing Nature Poems by Connie Colwell Miller and Jennifer Fandel. Poet in You. North Mankato, MN: Capstone, 2014. (2–4)

My School

Write sentences with your school's name. Make the first letter a capital letter. It might look like this:

NEWMAN

Newman is in New Orleans.

Elephants do not go to my school.

We take field trips.

My favorite class is math.

At recess we play volleyball.

Newman is a very good school.

Ready? Take 5!

Letter Detectives

My brother Brad broke my bright bracelet. Can you find a pattern? The letters *br* begin five of the seven words in the sentence.

Now it's your turn! Write a sentence using many other *br* words, such as these:

brick	broil	brave
bread	brush	brain
brake	brag	bridge
broom	bring	

Let's do another one! Here are the new words:

thief	brief	tie
relief	pie	tried
believe	cried	
chief	flies	

See the pattern? The letters *ie* appear in every word. Write a sentence using many of these *ie* words. You may use other *ie* words as well.

Ready? Take

LANGUAGE LINK

Complete Sentences
Spelling Patterns

LEARNING SETTING

Individual

DEPTH OF KNOWLEDGE

● ● ○ ○

SUPPLIES

Journal, pencil

STANDARDS

I can spell words by using spelling patterns.

I can write complete sentences.

LET'S EXPLORE MORE

This activity can be done on another day using other letter groupings such as *cl*, *tr*, or *sp*.

Spelling Queen by Marci Peschke. Kylie Jean. North Mankato, MN: Capstone, 2012. (2–3)

Pick up the Phone!

Ring! Ring! Mason, answer your phone. Wait a minute. Your phone doesn't ring. It honks!

Some phones ring. Some phones honk or beep. Some phones play a song.

You have a new phone. Choose a song for your ring tone. What is the song?

_____

Why is that the best song?

_____

_____.

Ready? Take **5!**

Celebrate!

We honor presidents on Presidents' Day, moms on Mother's Day, and dads on Father's Day. We celebrate our freedom on the Fourth of July. On Thanksgiving, we give thanks.

Hmm, nothing is on the calendar for today. Let's create a new holiday. Who or what shall we honor? At the top of your paper, write the name of this holiday.

In the first space, or plain, complete this sentence:

This holiday celebrates _____.

In the second plain, list foods for this holiday. In the third plain, write the games and activities for this celebration. In the fourth plain, describe the decorations. Here is an example for "Love an Animal Day!"

This holiday celebrates <u>all animals. We should take care of them</u>.

Food: animal crackers, honey (bears), peanuts (elephants)

Games and activities: go to a petting zoo, play "Duck, Duck, Goose"

Decorations: stuffed animals

Ready? Take 5!

LANGUAGE LINK

Informative Writing

LEARNING SETTING

Individual

DEPTH OF KNOWLEDGE

SUPPLIES

"Xplain" Your Writing Graphic Organizer (p. 184), journal, pencil

STANDARD

I can provide supporting details for a topic in informative writing.

LET'S EXPLORE MORE

Pick a Picture, Write an Opinion! by Kristen McCurry. Little Scribe. North Mankato, MN: Capstone, 2014. (1–2)

LANGUAGE LINK
Narrative Writing

LEARNING SETTING
Individual

DEPTH OF KNOWLEDGE

SUPPLIES
Journal, pencil

STANDARD
I can write narrative events in the correct order.

LET'S EXPLORE MORE
Transportation Zone (Sezries) by Peter Brady. North Mankato, MN: Capstone, 2012. (1–2)

Tessa's Present

Tessa's grandmother sends her a birthday present every year. It must travel many miles.

It first goes by boat to the nearest town.

It then goes by bus to the airport. The airplane flies over very tall mountains.

Next, the present is placed on a truck. The truck travels across the desert.

Finally, the present arrives on Tessa's doorstep.

This year, a very unusual event happened with the birthday present. It was really quite funny. If only the present could talk! No one would believe its story.

Write a funny adventure about Tessa's birthday present.

Ready? Take **5!**

Lost and Found

The school "lost and found" closet is so full. It is filled with many lost items. The principal needs your help. Can you identify these items? Here are the items:

baseball	fishing pole
black boot	colored pencils
yellow raincoat	butterfly net
princess crown	bag of seashells
joke book	ballet slipper
soccer ball	horseshoe
dog collar	torn backpack
melted chocolate bar	skateboard

Select four items. In front of the item, write the name of one person who could be the owner of the item. Remember to use an apostrophe and an *s*. Then give a reason why that item could belong to that person. Think of family and friends. Here is an example:

Kyle's horseshoe because he has a horse

Ready? Take

LANGUAGE LINK
Apostrophes

LEARNING SETTING
Individual

DEPTH OF KNOWLEDGE

SUPPLIES
Journal, pencil

STANDARD
I can use apostrophes in possessives.

LET'S EXPLORE MORE
The Electric Company presents a musical lesson on possession— "Good Old Apostrophe S"— available on YouTube.

SUPPLIES

Journal; pencil; copies of famous paintings such as *The Juggler* by Marc Chagall, *Starry Night* by Vincent van Gogh; *The Persistence of Memory* by Salvador Dalí, and *American Gothic* by Grant Wood (many can be accessed at The National Gallery of Art online)

STANDARD

I can support my opinion with reasons.

LET'S EXPLORE MORE

Step into the Painting: Have students use the painting as narrative story starters with many different perspectives. This could also make a great class book!

Art by Charlotte Guillain. Jobs If You Like… . Chicago, IL: Heinemann Library, 2013. (1–3)

Art Works

Look at this painting. Observe the many details. Start in the middle. Then, move your eyes around the painting. In a paragraph, answer these questions:

I would name this painting _____.

Next, list three reasons to support your answer.

1. _____

2. _____

3. _____

This painting makes me feel _____

because _____.

Ready? Take 5!

Object Art

An artist sees an apple. She then paints a bright red apple. She paints a real object. Another artist looks at an apple. He is feeling very angry at the moment. So he sees angry red lines. He paints bright red lines. Some artists paint objects. Other artists paint feelings and ideas inspired by objects.

Today, you will be an inspired artist. Look at any object in the room. Draw only one small part of the object. Next, look at another object. Draw one part of this object over the first object. You may add more lines, squares, or circles on or around your picture. You can even color your artwork, but use only one or two colors. On the back, sign your name and write and complete this sentence:

This picture reminds me of _____

because _____

_____

_____.

Hang your artwork together in a class art gallery.

....

Ready? Take 5!

LANGUAGE LINK
Opinion Writing

LEARNING SETTING
Individual

DEPTH OF KNOWLEDGE

SUPPLIES

Journal; pencil; copies of paintings such as *Composition IV* by Wassily Kandinsky, *Tableau I* by Piet Mondrian, *Number 1 (Lavender Mist)* by Jackson Pollock, *Interchange* by Willem de Kooning, and *April* by Kenneth Noland (many can be accessed at The National Gallery of Art online)

STANDARD

I can support my opinion with reasons.

LET'S EXPLORE MORE

Art-Rageous by Jessica Young. Finley Flowers. North Mankato, MN: Capstone, 2016. (2–3)

Students can create their own abstract artwork at The NGAkids Art Zone.

SUPPLIES

Brown paper bags, markers, googly eyes, yarn, scissors, buttons, glue, tape, ribbon, an assortment of materials

STANDARDS

I can describe people, places, things, and events with relevant details.

I can add drawings or details to a description to provide information.

LET'S EXPLORE MORE

Fun Things to Do with Cardboard Tubes by Marne Ventura. 10 Things to Do. North Mankato, MN: Capstone, 2015. (1–2)

Fun Things to Do with Paper Cups and Plates by Kara L. Laughlin. 10 Things to Do. North Mankato, MN: Capstone, 2015. (1–2)

Raven's Present

Raven's brother is having a birthday. Yum! Look at the cake. Wow! Look at the gifts. Gifts? Oh no! Raven forgot his gift. All she has is a brown paper bag. Help turn her bag into a great gift.

Use your journal to begin planning. Describe two or more ideas. Could it be part of a game? A puppet? A kite? Circle the best idea. Then have fun making the gift with the brown bag. Add or cut details as needed.

Ready? Take **5!**

The Sleeping Giant I

Quiet! The <u>mean</u> giant is sleeping in the <u>big</u> castle. Don't wake him. He can become very <u>angry</u>. Climb the <u>tall</u> steps. Squeak! That fourth step is very <u>loud</u>. Be very <u>still</u>. Listen! Did you hear something? No! Don't open that <u>huge</u> door!

Describing words, or adjectives, can change an entire story. First, create a numbered list from 1 to 7. Next to each number, write the underlined words in the story. These are adjectives. Next, swap each adjective for an antonym, or a word that means the opposite. Now, the story is so different! Share your stories with others!

Ready? Take

LANGUAGE LINK

Antonyms
Adjectives

LEARNING SETTING

Individual

DEPTH OF KNOWLEDGE

● ○ ○ ○

SUPPLIES

Journal, pencil

STANDARDS

I can identify antonyms of words.

I can use adjectives (describing words).

LET'S EXPLORE MORE

The Sleeping Giant II: Somebody did not listen. The door has been opened. The giant knows someone is there! Have students complete the rest of the narrative story. They may use the original version of the story or their revised version. Encourage students to share their ending with the class.

LANGUAGE LINK

Descriptive Writing

LEARNING SETTING

Collaborative

DEPTH OF KNOWLEDGE

SUPPLIES

Journal, colored pencils

STANDARDS

I can describe people, places, things, and events with relevant details.

I can add drawings or details to a description to provide information.

LET'S EXPLORE MORE

The National Fire Prevention Association (NFPA) provides games, comics, and coloring pages at the website for Sparky the Fire Dog, the NFPA's official mascot.

Find favorite NFL team mascots to color from Super Coloring's online NFL coloring pages.

Team Spirit

Go Lions! You can do it, Tigers! Let's score, Bears! Lions and tigers and bears? Oh my! What is going on? It's football season! Football, baseball, hockey, and soccer teams often have animal names and mascots.

"Go _____!" Your team is missing a name. Some players really like insect names. Others like animals, plants, or trees. Let's create one!

On your group's paper, write the name of your team.

Under the name, describe or draw your mascot.

Then, draw a uniform for your team using your team colors.

Create a picture for your team name.

Below the drawing, write a slogan for your team. For example, "Bee a winner!" could be the slogan for a team called the Bees.

Possible names: Giraffes, Flies, Wasps, Grasshoppers, Dragonflies, Crickets, Moths, Spiders, Kangaroos, Octopuses, Palms, Pines, Oaks

Ready? Take **5!**

The Neighbors of Building C

On First Avenue cars and trucks go rushing by.

The buildings stand tall. They reach to the sky.

You live on First Avenue in Building C. You live on the fifth floor. You have some very interesting neighbors. Who are they? What are they like? Number your paper from 1 to 5. For each number, fill in the blanks with a reason for your opinion.

1. Below you is _____. He is very talented

   because he _____.

2. Above you is _____. She can be very kind

   as she always _____.

3. Next door is _____. He is very helpful

   because _____.

4. Across the hall is _____. She is so healthy

   as she _____.

5. You enjoy living here because _____.

6. Who is your favorite neighbor? Explain why.

Ready? Take 5!

LANGUAGE LINK
Opinion Writing

LEARNING SETTING
Individual

DEPTH OF KNOWLEDGE
● ● ● ○

SUPPLIES
Journal, pencil

STANDARD
I can support my opinion with reasons.

LET'S EXPLORE MORE
My Hometown by Russell Griesmer. North Mankato, MN: Capstone, 2016. (1–4)

LANGUAGE LINK
Narrative Writing

LEARNING SETTING
Individual

DEPTH OF KNOWLEDGE

SUPPLIES
Journal, pencil

STANDARD
I can write narrative events in the correct order.

LET'S EXPLORE MORE

School Bus Safety: An informational writing prompt for another day is to have student groups make a list of things bus riders can do for a safe bus ride. As a follow-up they can also make posters to hang in the classroom or hallways.

Red, Yellow, Purple Lights

Mr. Coates, the bus driver, is driving your bus. You like Mr. Coates. He is very friendly. He is also a safe driver. He slows down for yellow lights. He stops at red lights. Wait a minute! There is a purple light flashing ahead! Write or draw the answer to these questions.

What does the purple light mean? (Your answers could be silly like these: *Everyone say purple!* OR *Take a cookie break!*)

What does Mr. Coates say or do at the purple light?

Ready? Take 5!

Broken Fairy Tales

Once upon a time, a witch put the gingerbread man in her oven. Hansel was too quick for her. He grabbed the handle and opened the oven. Out jumped the gingerbread man. He ran out the door and fell into a rabbit hole. The three bears heard him shout.

Hey! All the stories are mixed up. With a partner, complete the story from this point. Use other fairy tale people and places in your story.

Ready? Take 5!

LANGUAGE LINK
Narrative Writing

LEARNING SETTING
Pair

DEPTH OF KNOWLEDGE

SUPPLIES
Journal, pencil

STANDARD
I can write narrative events in the correct order.

LET'S EXPLORE MORE
Flip-Side Nursery Rhymes (Series) by Christopher Harbo. North Mankato, MN: Capstone, 2015. (PreK–2)

Little Red Riding Duck by Charlotte Guillain. Animal Fairy Tales. Chicago, IL: Heinemann Library, 2013. (PreK–2)

Writing Stories (Series) by Anita Ganeri. Chicago, IL: Heinemann Library, 2014. (1–3)

Conjunctions Compound Sentences

Pair

DEPTH OF KNOWLEDGE

SUPPLIES

Journal, pencil, assortment of worn children's book pages that will be cut up (ask your friends for books or check out garage sales), scissors, tape

STANDARDS

I can use conjunctions (connecting words).

I can use simple and compound sentences.

LET'S EXPLORE MORE

What Is a Conjunction? by Jennifer Fandel. Parts of Speech. North Mankato, MN: Capstone, 2013. (K–1)

Bridge Builders

A bridge joins one side of a road to the other side. Connecting words act like bridges. They can join simple sentences. This creates a compound sentence. Connecting words are words like *but, and, so, yet, nor,* and *for.*

It might look like this:

BUT

Jaz wants a bike for his birthday,  but his old bike works well.

Now it's your turn. Cut out four simple sentences from the printed materials. Swap two sentences with your partner. Tape two sentences together in your journal. Leave room for a connecting word between them. You should have two very strange compound sentences. Have fun reading your sentences to the class.

Ready? Take **5!**

Playtime in the Den

In Wildwood Forest, animals roam among the trees and bushes. Kita and Mari are there too. These two tiger cubs tumble and play together. Also, they watch their mother. She shows them safe places in the jungle. Here they can hide from their enemies. The cubs' mother teaches them to hunt. They will soon hunt for their own food. After a long day, they return to their den and sleep.

You don't live in a den like a tiger. You live in a house. But, like wild animals, you also can learn from others. What can you learn from them? On your paper, write the name of a person. Next, write or draw two things you can learn from this person.

Ready? Take

LANGUAGE LINK

Informative Writing

LEARNING SETTING

Individual

DEPTH OF KNOWLEDGE

SUPPLIES

Journal, pencil

STANDARD

I can provide supporting details for a topic in informative writing.

LET'S EXPLORE MORE

Manners at Home by Sian Smith. Oh, Behave! Chicago, IL: Heinemann Library, 2013. (PreK–1)

Basil the Bear Cub by Janey Louise Jones. Superfairies. North Mankato, MN: Capstone, 2016. (K–3)

LANGUAGE LINK
Narrative Writing

LEARNING SETTING
Individual

DEPTH OF KNOWLEDGE
● ● ● ●

SUPPLIES
Journal, pencil

STANDARD
I can write narrative events in the correct order.

LET'S EXPLORE MORE
Adventure Stories by Anita Ganeri. Writing Stories. Chicago, IL: Heinemann Library, 2014. (1–3)

A Story in Pictures

Try and read this picture story.

Now read this same story with words.

One sunny day we hiked to the mountains. Oh no! Look! There are bear tracks. We were so scared. Just then, from a bush came a small baby deer. We felt happy and safe! We set up our tent and fell fast asleep.

The first story is written with pictures. The second story is written with words. Before letters of the alphabet were invented, people only wrote with pictures. These pictures can still be seen in old caves. Now, it's your turn. Write a very short story in pictures. You will need a beginning, a middle, and an end—just like the example.

Share your story with others. Here is a question for your journal: What is the main problem with a story in pictures?

Ready? Take

Coming Soon!

The Biddle Town Nature Center has just been built. In one week, it will open. Wait a minute! The "Get to Know This Animal" cards are missing! Visitors need these. They provide information about animals, plants, and insects in the park. Hurry! We must make new cards. Each group will take one card. Look at the picture closely. Put your heads together! What does your group already know about this animal or insect? One person will be the recorder. The recorder will list this information on the back of the card. Then check other sources for more information. Add these facts to the list on the card.

Ready? Take

LANGUAGE LINK

Research

LEARNING SETTING

Collaborative

DEPTH OF KNOWLEDGE

SUPPLIES

Note cards with an animal picture affixed to one side (one per group), pencil, pen

STANDARD

I can participate in shared research and writing projects (e.g., read a number of books on a single topic to produce a report; record science observations).

LET'S EXPLORE MORE

Students can combine their information into a slideshow or turn it into a booklet.

Animals by Charlotte Guillain. Jobs If You Like .... Chicago, IL: Heinemann Library, 2013. (1–3)

Insects by Martha E. H. Rustad. Smithsonian Little Explorer. North Mankato, MN: Capstone, 2015. (1–2)

SUPPLIES

Journal, pencil, "Xplain" Your Writing Graphic Organizer (p. 184)

STANDARD

I can capitalize places, names, dates, and holidays.

LET'S EXPLORE MORE

Capital letters and more are something to sing about in "The Sentence Song!" by Scratch Garden on YouTube.

Superstars

Big letters are superstars in a sentence. They are called capital letters, and they are very pushy. They knock little letters out of the way. They must be first in line in a sentence. They also want their own names. They will never be *girl* or *boy*. They must be Jaiden or James. They won't be *town* or *city*. They must be New York or Maryville.

On your "Xplain" sheet, write "Cities and States" in the number 1 space, or plain. In the number 2 space, write "Days or Months." In the number 3 space, write "People's Names." In the number 4 space, write "Holidays." In each space, write or draw items for that category that begin with a capital letter.

Ready? Take

That's a Bunch!

One lion, two lions, three lions. Oh wow! It's a whole pride of lions! One bird, two birds, three birds. Look! It's a flock of birds! A *flock* is a whole bunch of birds in one group. A *den* is a whole bunch of lions. (Look out!) A *class* is a whole bunch of students. *Flock*, *den*, and *class* are collective nouns. They collect more than one object. Here are more collective nouns.

team (players)	flock (birds)
troop (soldiers)	crowd (people)
swarm (butterflies)	herd (cows, elephants)
orchard (fruit trees)	litter (kittens)
galaxy (stars and planets)	pack (rats, wolves)
batch (cookies)	string (ponies)

Select two of these collective nouns. On your paper, write the noun. What does it look like? Draw a picture of each collective noun.

Ready? Take

LANGUAGE LINK
Collective Nouns

LEARNING SETTING
Individual

DEPTH OF KNOWLEDGE
● ○ ○ ○

SUPPLIES
Journal, colored pencils

STANDARD
I can use collective nouns.

LET'S EXPLORE MORE
Animals That Live in Groups by Kelsi Turner Tjernagel. Learn about Animal Behavior. North Mankato, MN: Capstone, 2013. (1–2)

SUPPLIES

Journal, pencil, "Xplain" Your Writing Graphic Organizer (p. 184)

STANDARD

I can provide supporting details for a topic in informative writing.

LET'S EXPLORE MORE

Party Time!: This informational writing prompt can be used on other days with themes like bugs, the circus, under the sea, etc. Students can work in groups to create and plan a party.

Space Party

It's party time! Let's pick a theme. We could have a princess party. A turtle party is also fun. What about a bug party or a party with a doll, train, or famous mouse theme? I know! Let's have a space party!

Let's make a list. Hmm, what about food? Big round lollipops for planets, sandwiches cut into stars, star fruit cut into slices, moon rocks (drop cookies). What will people drink? What will they do? Let's make plans! With a partner, write the theme of your party at the top of your "Xplain" sheet. Next, fill in each space, or plain, with the following:

Plain 1: Foods

Plain 2: Drinks

Plain 3: Games and Activities

Plain 4: Decorations

Think of many fun ideas for your party!

Ready? Take **5!**

The Perfect Tree House

It is Saturday morning. Charlie wants a quiet, peaceful day. Oh no! Why is it so noisy? Charlie's baby sister Claire is crying. Charlie's older brother Will is dribbling a basketball in his room. Charlie's father is talking on his cell phone. Charlie's grandmother is clanging pots and pans in the kitchen. Charlie's neighbors have barking dogs. Charlie covered his ears. "I need a quiet place," he moaned.

Charlie needs your help. Design a quiet place for Charlie high in a tree. First, draw this house. Add details for blocking sound. Under the picture, begin a paragraph with this sentence: *Charlie's tree house is very quiet.* Next, write three sentences describing Charlie's house and why it is so quiet. Then, write one last sentence about this perfect tree house. This sentence brings the paragraph to a close.

Ready? Take **5!**

LANGUAGE LINK
Descriptive Writing

LEARNING SETTING
Individual

DEPTH OF KNOWLEDGE

SUPPLIES
Journal, pencil

STANDARDS
I can describe people, places, things, and events with relevant details.

I can add drawings or details to a description to provide information.

LET'S EXPLORE MORE
Welcome to the Treehouse by Art Baltazar and Franco. DC Comics Tiny Titans. North Mankato, MN: Capstone, 2013. (1–2)

LANGUAGE LINK
Narrative Writing

LEARNING SETTING
Individual

DEPTH OF KNOWLEDGE

SUPPLIES
Journal, pencil

STANDARD
I can write narrative events in the correct order.

LET'S EXPLORE MORE
California Sea Lions by Megan C. Peterson. Marine Mammals. North Mankato, MN: Capstone, 2013. (K–1)

Lunch with a Sea Lion

A baby sea lion is all alone. No other pups are around. Who will play with him? Fill in the blanks to complete the story.

"Not me," said the shrimp. "You might eat me for lunch."

"Not me," said the whale. "I must _____

_____.

(Finish the sentence.)

"Not me," said the octopus. "I have _____

_____.

(Finish the sentence.)

"Not me," said the fish. "I need to _____

_____.

(Finish the sentence.)

The pup was so sad. But then he heard a voice.

"I will play with you," said the _____

_____.

(Finish the sentence.)

And here is what they did. Complete the story.

Ready? Take 5!

Who Stole the Pie?

Aunt Peekie took a peach pie out of the oven. Eight friends were coming for dinner. Each person would enjoy one piece of pie. Aunt Peekie needed flowers for her table. She went outside to her garden and snipped and clipped her flowers. And then she went back inside. Oh no! The pie plate is empty!

"Did you steal my pie?" Aunt Peekie shouted.

Mr. Period spoke first. "I did not steal the pie. I only ate two slices."

Aunt Peekie stared at Ms. Question Mark.

"Why are you looking at me? Do I look like a thief? Didn't I only eat two slices? So what?"

Aunt Peekie then looked at Mr. Exclamation Point.

"No! Don't look at me! I'm not a thief! I'm an honest person! I only ate two slices!"

Slowly, they all turned and looked at Mr. Comma.

"No, I'm not a thief, but I was hungry. Aunt Peekie, I only ate two slices."

So, who stole the pie? Solve this mystery. Write the answer in your journal. Use a comma, a question mark, an exclamation point, and a period in your answer.

Ready? Take

Chapter Four: The Prompts | 115

LANGUAGE LINK
Punctuation

LEARNING SETTING
Individual

DEPTH OF KNOWLEDGE

 ●●●○

SUPPLIES

Journal, pencil

STANDARD

I can use end punctuation for sentences.

LET'S EXPLORE MORE

Whatever says mark: Knowing and Using Punctuation by Terry Collins. Language on the Loose. North Mankato, MN: Capstone, 2014. (2–4)

Watch and listen to "The Punctuation People: Ms. Exclamation" on YouTube.

LANGUAGE LINK
Opinion Writing

LEARNING SETTING
Individual

DEPTH OF KNOWLEDGE

SUPPLIES

Journal, pencil

STANDARD

I can support my opinion
with reasons.

LET'S EXPLORE MORE

Have students write thank-you
cards to their special "stars."

Wishing on a Star

High in the sky, many stars twinkle. But there is another
kind of star. Stars are also in our homes, schools, and
cities. Stars do something nice for others. Stars walk
dogs for the sick. They help with homework. Stars pick
up trash. They say "Please" and "Thank you." Think of
a star. Next, write this sentence on a star you draw in
your journal:

_____

is a star because _____

_____.

Next, write one more sentence about this star:

_____.

Ready? Take 5!

Book Week

Let's celebrate our favorite book characters! Choose a book character. Invite this character to lunch.

First, make an invitation. Create a shape for the invitation. Winnie the Pooh would like a honey pot card. Angelina Ballerina might like a ballet slipper. Other characters might like a dog collar, a purple crayon or purse, or maybe a train, pink sweets, or an umbrella.

Next, write on the card. Invite people to your party. Include the day of the party (like May 2) and the time (like 2:00 p.m.). What food will you serve? What food would this character eat? Add these details to the invitation. Example: What would a dragon eat? Fire-roasted potatoes, flaming steaks, and toasted marshmallows! Be creative!

Ready? Take

LANGUAGE LINK
Descriptive Writing

LEARNING SETTING
Individual

DEPTH OF KNOWLEDGE

SUPPLIES

Scissors, construction paper, colored pencils, or a computerized card maker

STANDARD

I can add drawings or details to a description to provide information.

LET'S EXPLORE MORE

Create a book collage using the students' products.

Kylie Jean Party Craft Queen by Marci Peschke and Marne Ventura. Kylie Jean Craft Queen. North Mankato, MN: Capstone, 2014. (2–3)

SUPPLIES
Journal, pencil

STANDARDS
I can write narrative events in the correct order.

I can determine differences in meaning of similar verbs and adjectives.

LET'S EXPLORE MORE

A Summer Day II: Students can continue the summer vacation narrative story of Drey and Monae. What new adventures will they encounter? They should use the same word bank.

Funny Stories by Anita Ganeri. Writing Stories. Chicago, IL: Heinemann Library, 2014. (1–3)

A Summer Day I

On the first day of summer, Drey and his sister Monae jumped on their bikes. They were excited and ready for adventure. Four hours later, they returned home.

"You won't believe it!" Monae told her mother.

"It was awesome!" Drey added. "You will not believe this!"

Continue this story using words the characters would say. But do not use the verb *said.* Use other speaking words from the word bank for this mysterious story.

Word Bank

added	cried	sighed
agreed	explained	snapped
answered	gasped	snarled
argued	howled	spoke
asked	moaned	squealed
blurted	promised	told
called	roared	wailed
chuckled	screamed	whispered

Ready? Take 5!

Missing Sounds

The words *pit* and *sit* rhyme. They sound alike. They almost look alike. Only the first letter is not the same. *Bed* and *red* also rhyme. What about *land* and *wand*? HEY! Shouldn't they rhyme? Just because word endings look alike doesn't mean they always sound alike.

Say these pairs of words slowly:

want/ant	are/bare	was/gas
were/here	lose/nose	pour/hour
warm/arm	put/but	hear/bear

Your task: Choose two pairs of words, like *was* and *gas*. Write one sentence for each pair of words. A sentence must have a verb. The first word in each pair is the verb. It might look like this:

I did not *hear* the *bear*.

Ready? Take

LANGUAGE LINK

Spelling Patterns
Complete Sentences

LEARNING SETTING

Individual

DEPTH OF KNOWLEDGE

SUPPLIES

Paper and pencil

STANDARDS

I can spell simple words by sounding them out.

I can produce complete sentences in class activities.

LET'S EXPLORE MORE

Unrhymed Poetry Time: Students might like the additional challenge of turning their sentences into a poem. Discuss poems written in free verse and provide examples. Students can brainstorm to add more similarly spelled words (*bone/one*) to their lists and create new (often silly) sentences for their poems.

> What does he WANT
> This giant ANT?
> Can he eat a BONE?
> Well, he might eat ONE.

It Doesn't Need to Rhyme, Katie Woo by Fran Manushkin. Katie Woo: Star Writer. North Mankato, MN: Capstone, 2014. (K–2)

LANGUAGE LINK

Sorting

LEARNING SETTING

Pair

DEPTH OF KNOWLEDGE

● ○ ○ ○

SUPPLIES

Journal, colored pencils

STANDARD

I can sort common words or objects into categories.

LET'S EXPLORE MORE

Patterns Outside by Daniel Nunn. Math Every Day. Chicago, IL: Heinemann Library, 2012. (PreK–K)

Students can help Cookie Monster find the patterns in "The Hungry Games" at the PBS Kids website.

Make a Pattern

Many things have a pattern. Look at this pattern.

 _____

The circle and triangle make a pattern. What would go after the last triangle? A circle!

Here is another pattern:

1 2 3 4 1 2 ___ 4

What number is missing? The 3! How do you know? It's a pattern.

Now it's your turn. Write or draw two different patterns in your journal. These can be words, shapes, numbers, or colors. Then swap your journal with a partner. Find the patterns!

Ready? Take **5!**

Martin's Dream

Martin Luther King Jr. was a great leader, but he was sad. He did not like fighting. He did not like name-calling. He wanted peace for all people. One day, he spoke about a dream. His dream was about peace. In his dream, everyone liked each other. Boys and girls all got along. People of different backgrounds all got along. They did not fight. This was his dream.

What is your dream? Draw two large clouds. In each cloud, describe or draw one dream. This dream is not about you. Begin with these words:

I have a dream.

_____

It might look like this:

I have a dream. It is a kind world. We would not call each other names.

I have a dream. The ocean would be clean. It would not have trash.

....

Ready? Take 

LANGUAGE LINK
Descriptive Writing

LEARNING SETTING
Individual

DEPTH OF KNOWLEDGE

SUPPLIES

Journal, pencil

STANDARD

I can describe people, places, things, and events with relevant details.

LET'S EXPLORE MORE

Peace: Explain to students that Dr. King looked for peaceful solutions to problems. He did not believe in violence. In the middle of a piece of paper, students can write or draw what the word *peace* means to them. They can add one or more pictures around the word to describe what peace looks like to them. These papers can be hung together in the class art gallery.

Martin Luther King Jr. by Riley Flynn. Great African-Americans. North Mankato, MN: Capstone, 2014. (K–1)

LANGUAGE LINK
Adjectives

LEARNING SETTING
Individual

DEPTH OF KNOWLEDGE
● ○ ○ ○

SUPPLIES
Construction paper, markers, scissors

STANDARD
I can use adjectives
(describing words).

LET'S EXPLORE MORE
*Describing Words: Adjectives,
Adverbs, and Prepositions* by
Anita Ganeri. Getting to Grips
with Grammar. Chicago, IL:
Heinemann Library, 2012. (1–3)

A Hat Full of Adjectives by Bette
Blaisdell. Words I Know. North
Mankato, MN: Capstone, 2014. (1–2)

Mr. Clover's Fruit Stand

Mr. Clover's fruit stand sits on the corner. Here, he sells many kinds of fruit. But he has a problem. People are walking by his stand. They are not buying any fruit. He is afraid the fruit will rot. Let's help Mr. Clover! Choose one fruit. Draw and cut out the fruit. Then, write one or more adjectives before the fruit's name. Make it sound very tasty! It might look like this:

Tart, juicy cherries   *Yellow, sour lemons*

Here are some of the fruits at Mr. Clover's fruit stand:

apples	guava	peaches
apricots	jujube	pears
bananas	kiwis	pineapples
blueberries	limes	plums
coconuts	melons	raspberries
figs	oranges	strawberries
grapes	papaya	

Hang all the fruit signs together. Put them under a big sign titled "Mr. Clover's Fruit Stand."

Ready? Take

I See Colors

I see something green! Look around the room. So many colors can be seen! Make four lists. At the top of each, write the colors "red," "green," "blue," and "black." Write or draw the objects you see in the correct list.

Ready? Take  *5!*

Mixed-up Art

Look at the picture. Do you see an apple? Do you see a car? The artists did not always want real objects in their pictures. The artists wanted colors and shapes and lines. Make your own picture. Pull four shapes from the bag. Glue them together on the page. At the top of the page, give the picture a name. Below the picture, copy this sentence and fill in the blank. Write additional sentences to describe your picture:

This picture is about _____

_____.

It might read like this:

This picture is about fall. Leaves fall to the ground. They change colors.

Ready? Take 5!

The Long Train Ride

You are going on a long train ride. The train will stop at four places. These stops are not alike. The train could stop at places like this: the mountains, your grandmother's house, a park, a desert, a zoo, a circus, a playground, or a big city. Where will you stop?

Using your "Xplain" sheet, draw your four stops. At the top of each one, write the name of the stop like "My friend's house."

On the back of the page, complete this sentence:

My favorite stop is _____

because _____

_____.

Ready? Take

LANGUAGE LINK
Opinion Writing

LEARNING SETTING
Individual

DEPTH OF KNOWLEDGE
● ● ○ ○

SUPPLIES
Journal, colored pencils, "Xplain" Your Writing Graphic Organizer (p. 184)

STANDARDS
I can support my opinion with reasons.

I can add drawings or details to a description to provide information.

LET'S EXPLORE MORE
Passenger Trains by Nikki Bruno Clapper. All Aboard! North Mankato, MN: Capstone, 2016. (K–1)

LANGUAGE LINK

Sentences

LEARNING SETTING

Individual

DEPTH OF KNOWLEDGE

SUPPLIES

Journal, pencil

STANDARD

I can produce complete sentences in class activities.

LET'S EXPLORE MORE

The Fancy Octopus by Cari Meister. Stone Arch Readers. North Mankato, MN: Capstone, 2012. (2–3)

Octopuses by Anna Claybourne. Animal Abilities. Chicago, IL: Heinemann Library, 2014. (2–4)

The Octopus

Something is wrong. Mazee was tired last night. She fell asleep writing her science report. The periods are in the wrong place! Help Mazee. Rewrite the report with complete sentences.

In the deep blue water. An octopus skims across. The bottom of the ocean. Its sharp beak. Pulls open clamshells. The meat of a clam. Makes a yummy snack. They can escape their enemies. With a big squirt of black ink. They can also change colors. And blend in with the sand. Many people love. To eat octopus. How about you?

Ready? Take

Oh No, Terrick!

Terrick can be so much trouble. Things always happen to him. Oh no, Terrick! What have you done?

I went fishing, but I fell into the lake!

I need a new basketball because I lost mine at the park.

Write or draw the rest of each sentence. Look at the connecting word carefully. It will lead the way.

Oh no, Terrick! What have you done?

I _____, but it _____.

Oh no, Terrick! What have you done?

I _____, and they _____.

Oh no, Terrick! What have you done?

I _____, so he _____.

Oh no, Terrick! What have you done?

I _____ because no one _____.

Ready? Take 5!

DEPTH OF KNOWLEDGE

SUPPLIES

Journal, colored pencils

STANDARD

I can use simple and compound sentences.

LET'S EXPLORE MORE

Grouping Words: Sentences by Anita Ganeri. Getting to Grips with Grammar. Chicago, IL: Heinemann Library, 2012. (1–3)

Select the correct conjunction in the "Conjunction Game for Kids" on the Fun English Games website.

LANGUAGE LINK
Interrogatives

LEARNING SETTING
Individual

DEPTH OF KNOWLEDGE

● ○ ○ ○

SUPPLIES

Journal, pencil, assortment of pictures (cut from magazines, brought from home, found on the Internet)

STANDARD

I can use question words.

LET'S EXPLORE MORE

Picture Stories: Students can use the photograph as a narrative story starter or poem starter. They can even pair with a partner and use two photographs in a combined product.

Photographs by Isabel Thomas. Start with Art. Chicago, IL: Heinemann Library, 2012. (K–2)

Pick a Picture, Write a Poem! by Kristen McCurry. Little Scribe. North Mankato, MN: Capstone, 2014. (1–2)

Say Cheese!

Snap! Look closely at the picture in front of you. You have many questions about this picture. Glue the picture into your journal. Under the picture, write three questions about your picture.

A question might look like this:

Why are the people laughing?

Share your pictures and questions with others in the class.

Ready? Take 5!

The Root Word Game

Many things can change. Words can change, too. Add more letters to a word. What happens? New words are made. Look at the word *paint*. Let's add *-er, -ed, -ing,* and *-s* to the end of the word.

It might look like this:

The painter painted the painting with his paints.

Wow! That is a mouthful! Let's do the same! Turn up a card from the first pile. This is the root word like *paint*. Turn up a card from the second pile. This is the word part pile. It has parts like *-er*. Will the two cards together make a new word? Yes! Then set both cards aside. Not a word? Then slip both cards back into their piles. Let's try again. Continue playing the Root Word Game. See how many new words can be made.

Ready? Take

LANGUAGE LINK
Roots Words
Suffixes

LEARNING SETTING
Collaborative

DEPTH OF KNOWLEDGE
● ● ○ ○

SUPPLIES

Two sets of cards per group: one set (one color) has root words on them like *look, jump, run, strong, care, tall, near, pull, sleep, train, teach, want, friend*; the second set (a different color) has suffixes like *-er, -y, -ly, -ful, -s, -es, -ed, -ing, -less*

STANDARDS

I can identify inflectional forms of a root word (*look: looks, looked, looking*).

I can use prefixes and/or suffixes to figure out word meanings.

LET'S EXPLORE MORE

Take a swing at the correct suffix in "Base Word Baseball" on the Tutoring for Tots website.

Complete each puzzle in the interactive activity "Matching Suffixes" on the Big Brown Bear website.

SUPPLIES

Cards or slips of paper with these antonyms: up/down, big/little, light/dark, close/open, cold/hot, right/wrong, come/go, dry/wet, easy/hard, early/late, false/true, fast/slow

STANDARD

I can identify antonyms of words.

LET'S EXPLORE MORE

Before and After by Joy Frisch-Schmoll. Exploring Opposites. North Mankato, MN: Capstone, 2013. (K–1)

Eddie and Ellie's Opposites (Series) by Daniel Nunn. Chicago, IL: Heinemann Library, 2014. (PreK–K)

Listen and watch "The Opposites Song" on the KidsTV123 YouTube channel.

SNAP!

Let's all snap our fingers. Snap! Now, we are ready to begin.

The first person turns up a card from the pile. Each card has two words. The two words are opposite in meaning. They are called *antonyms*. This player calls out the first word. Can the player to the left say the opposite word? *Yes*? Then the first player snaps her fingers. This means the player is correct. No antonym and no snap? Then the next player tries. Continue around the circle. After the right word is "snapped up," the next player picks a new card and the play begins again.

Ready? Take **5!**

The Mixed-up Elephant

Sound out the silly words in this poem by Laura Richards.

Eletelephony by Laura Elizabeth Richards

Once there was an elephant,
Who tried to use the telephant—
No! No! I mean an elephone
Who tried to use the telephone—
(Dear me! I am not certain quite
That even now I've got it right.)
Howe'er it was, he got his trunk
Entangled in the telephunk;
The more he tried to get it free,
The louder buzzed the telephee—
(I fear I'd better drop the song
Of elephop and telephong!)

Who has heard of a *telephee* or *elephop*? The author wrote a funny poem with silly words. There is no picture for this poem. The author is so sad! Let's draw a picture for this poem. Draw with a pencil first. Then add color to the picture.

Ready? Take **5!**

LANGUAGE LINK
Descriptive Writing

LEARNING SETTING
Individual

DEPTH OF KNOWLEDGE
● ◐ ◯ ◯

SUPPLIES
Journal, pencil, colored pencils

STANDARD
I can add drawings or details to a description to provide information.

LET'S EXPLORE MORE
Learning About Poems by Martha E. H. Rustad. North Mankato, MN: Capstone, 2015. (K–1)

Sing-Along Silly Songs (Series) by Steven Anderson. North Mankato, MN: Cantata Learning, 2016. (1–3)

Tickles, Pickles, and Floofing Persnickles: Reading and Writing Nonsense Poems by Blake Hoena, Catherine Ipcizade, and Connie Colwell Miller. North Mankato, MN: Capstone, 2014. (2–4)

LANGUAGE LINK
Narrative Writing

LEARNING SETTING
Individual

DEPTH OF KNOWLEDGE

SUPPLIES

Journal, pencil

STANDARD

I can write narrative events in the correct order.

LET'S EXPLORE MORE

What Happens Next, Katie?: Writing a Narrative with Katie Woo by Fran Manushkin. Katie Woo: Star Writer. North Mankato, MN: Capstone, 2014. (K–2)

The River Town Rat Race

Ready, set, go! Off the rats go in the first River Town Rat Race. They are running so fast! The finish line is two miles away at River Town Wharf. The first rat there will win. Wait a minute! Rat one is getting into a taxi. Rat two is on a skateboard. Rat three is taking a bus. Uh-oh! We made a mistake. We did not write any rules. Before next year's race, we need some rules. On your paper, write three important rules for the River Town Rat Race.

Ready? Take 5!

Give Me a Hand!

Look closely at your palm. Trace the many lines with your finger. Some run all the way across.

Turn your hand over and trace around it onto your paper. This will be your palm. Use a pencil to copy some of the lines of your palm onto the picture. Go across the fingers and down the hand. Your palm is now broken into smaller parts. Color each part a different color. Need more colors? Blend some of the colors. Also, you can use a darker or lighter shade of one color.

Count the number of colors. Above the handprint write "Give Me a Hand." Under the handprint, make a list. The list will equal the number of colors. Write nice things about yourself. Here are some ideas:

Good friend

Likes to read books

Smiles a lot

Has a dog named Buddy

Can sing 100 songs

Plays the piano

Sister

Loves ice cream

Ready? Take 5!

LANGUAGE LINK
Descriptive Writing

LEARNING SETTING
Individual

DEPTH OF KNOWLEDGE
● ● ○ ○

SUPPLIES
Journal, pencil, colored pencils

STANDARDS
I can describe people, places, things, and events with relevant details.

I can add drawings or details to a description to provide information.

LET'S EXPLORE MORE
Celebrating Differences (Series) by Melissa Higgins. North Mankato, MN: Capstone, 2012. (K–1)

LANGUAGE LINK
Research

LEARNING SETTING
Collaborative

DEPTH OF KNOWLEDGE

SUPPLIES

School yearbook or school's website, paper, pencils, paper cut into quarter sections, stapler, hole punch, ribbon, other items to bind/decorate a book

STANDARD

I can participate in research and writing projects with my classmates.

LET'S EXPLORE MORE

Students can turn their responses into a slideshow using their own voices with the app Shadow Puppet Edu, available at the iTunes App Store.

How Books Are Made by Martha E. H. Rustad. Wonderful World of Reading. North Mankato, MN: Capstone, 2013. (K–1)

The Parts of a Book by Martha E. H. Rustad. Wonderful World of Reading. North Mankato, MN: Capstone, 2013. (K–1)

This Is MY School

Is a gas station a school? No! It doesn't have books.

Is a park a school? No! It doesn't have a bus driver.

Is a beach a school? No! It doesn't have a bathroom.

"You Can't Have a School Without _____"

This is the title of your group book. There are many people, places, objects, and things in a school. Think of one thing a school needs. At the top of your paper, write this title but fill in the blank. Below the title, draw your idea. Brainstorm together with your group. Also, use other resources. For example, does your school have a website? A school yearbook? Next, put all the group's ideas together in one book. Don't forget a title page. Staple the pages together or be creative. Punch holes and run ribbon or string through the holes. Share your book with other groups. How are they different?

Ready? Take **5!**

All About Animals

Let's write a book about animals. First, you and a partner will select one animal. What about a donkey, a deer, or a titmouse? What about a woodpecker, an octopus, a cow, or a rattlesnake? So many choices! Look through books or on the Internet for information to complete each sentence. You can also add drawings. Then, place all the information together. Make a book or maybe a slideshow on the computer and share with others.

They have _____.

They look like _____.

They live in _____.

They like to eat _____.

They need _____.

They can be very _____.

Ready? Take 5!

LANGUAGE LINK

Research

LEARNING SETTING

Pair

DEPTH OF KNOWLEDGE

● ● ● ●

SUPPLIES

Nonfiction books on animals or websites such as *National Geographic*, paper, pencil, colored pencils

STANDARD

I can participate in research and writing projects with my classmates.

LET'S EXPLORE MORE

Animals by Charlotte Guillain. Jobs If You Like .... Chicago, IL: Heinemann Library, 2013. (1–3)

Animals All Day! (Series) by Joanne Ruelos Diaz. North Mankato, MN: Capstone, 2015. (K–2)

SUPPLIES

Journal, colored pencils, pencil

STANDARDS

I can describe people, places, things, and events with relevant details.

I can add drawings or details to a description to provide information.

LET'S EXPLORE MORE

The Runaway Sock II: What happened to the sock? On another day, continue the adventure of this narrative story. Where did it go, and what did it do? Was it found? Who found it? How did it come back? Students should be encouraged to use details in their stories.

Describing Words: Adjectives, Adverbs, and Prepositions by Anita Ganeri. Getting to Grips with Grammar. Chicago, IL: Heinemann Library, 2012. (1–3)

The Runaway Sock I

Oh, no! Not again! There is only one sock in the dryer. Is the other one in the washing machine? No, nothing is there. It must have run away. You need a missing sock sign. Describe your sock. Maybe someone will find it.

At the top of the sign write "Missing: One Sock." Then draw your sock. Make it a little like you. Think about these ideas:

Does it sparkle and glitter?

Is it camouflage?

Does it have holes in it?

What colors are on it?

Is there a pattern to the colors?

Does it have stripes along the top?

Are there animal faces on it?

Does it have toes?

Is it a sport sock with a team name?

Under the drawing, write three sentences to describe the sock.

Ready? Take 5!

Auntie Annie's Diner

Your Aunt Annie is opening a new diner. She has named it Annie's All-Day Diner. It serves breakfast, lunch, and dinner. Everything is in place. The doors will soon open. But there's just one problem. Aunt Annie does not have a kid's menu.

A menu is a list of foods. This is your task. Draw a front cover for a kid's menu. Inside, list four items. Make each item sound yummy! You will need describing words. These are called *adjectives*. Here are four examples:

cheesy macaroni

crunchy carrot sticks

spicy, glazed chicken wings

fizzy, fruity, ice-cold smoothie

Ready? Take

LANGUAGE LINK
Adjectives

LEARNING SETTING
Individual

DEPTH OF KNOWLEDGE
● ● ◐ ◐

SUPPLIES

Paper, different colors or patterns, colored pencils

STANDARD

I can use adjectives (describing words).

LET'S EXPLORE MORE

Aunt Annie: Aunt Annie is very grateful for the help. Have students write a thank-you note from Aunt Annie. Encourage them to use adjectives in their response. Here is an example: "You are a truly talented person. My cute and colorful children's menu is the best!"

Reading Is Everywhere by Martha E. H. Rustad. Wonderful World of Reading. North Mankato, MN: Capstone, 2013. (K–1)

What Is an Adjective? by Jennifer Fandel. Parts of Speech. North Mankato, MN: Capstone, 2013. (K–1)

The amusing adjective song "Paint the Way" from Grammaropolis on YouTube rhythmically explains adjectives, though it is a bit advanced in some sections.

LANGUAGE LINK
Prefixes
Informative Writing

LEARNING SETTING
Individual

DEPTH OF KNOWLEDGE

● ● ○ ○

SUPPLIES

Journal, pencil

STANDARD

I can use prefixes to figure out word meanings.

LET'S EXPLORE MORE

Write a "Re" Story: Students can use many of the words added to their lists or from a class list of "re" words to write a narrative piece.

Not Again!

Ms. Recardo entered her second-grade classroom with a stack of papers.

"OK, students, it is time to regroup. We must rewrite our stories. They need reworking. Some had many mistakes. Let's all redo our papers."

Make a list of each of these "re" words. Draw a line through "re." "Re" means "do again." Beside each word, write "again." List other "re" words. It will look like this:

R̶eword again.   R̶emove again.

Next, answer this question: How can students become better writers? Write or draw two possible answers. Use "re" words in your answer.

Ready? Take 5!

How to Ride an Elephant

LANGUAGE LINK
Informative Writing

LEARNING SETTING
Individual

DEPTH OF KNOWLEDGE
● ● ○ ○

SUPPLIES

Journal, pencil, "Xplain" Your
Writing Graphic Organizer (p. 184)

STANDARD

I can provide supporting details
for a topic in informative writing.

LET'S EXPLORE MORE

How Do You Do That?: On
another day, students can address
this prompt again but using real
events. They can use their "Xplain"
sheet to tell how to perform a task
in four steps like riding a bike, baking
cupcakes, or playing the piano.

Amazing Elephants by Charlotte
Guillain. Walk on the Wild
Side. Chicago, IL: Heinemann
Library, 2014. (2–4)

Elephants Are Awesome! by
Martha E. H. Rustad. Awesome
African Animals! North Mankato,
MN: Capstone, 2015. (1–2)

Pack your bags! Grab your camera! We're going on a
safari. A *safari* is a journey through trees, bushes, and
plains. People on a safari look for lions, elephants, and
tigers. Look up ahead! It's an elephant. Let's go for a
ride. Hmm, let's think about this. How DO you ride an
elephant? Using your "Xplain" sheet, explain or draw this
task in four easy steps. Begin with plain 1.

Ready? Take **5!**

LANGUAGE LINK
Informative Writing

LEARNING SETTING
Individual

DEPTH OF KNOWLEDGE

SUPPLIES

Journal, pencil

STANDARD

I can provide supporting details for a topic in informative writing.

LET'S EXPLORE MORE

Valentine Cards: Students can create Valentine cards with lots of details for a helper in the school or a family member.

A Short History of Valentine's Day by Sally Lee. Holiday Histories. North Mankato, MN: Capstone, 2016. (K–1)

Will You Be My Valentine?

On Valentine's Day many people give cards to friends and family. A card is nice, but we can do something nice for others every day of the year.

We can water the plants.

We can feed the neighbor's dog.

We can take out the garbage.

We can draw get-well cards for friends and family.

What else can we do? In your journal, write four more ideas.

Ready? Take 5!

Easy as PIE

The three little pigs did not get along. One said, "We should build a house with sticks." The second pig said, "We should build our house with straw." The third pig said, "You are both wrong! We should build our house with bricks."

They all had strong opinions. An *opinion* is a person's view or belief. People have different opinions on many topics. The three little pigs all had a different opinion.

Your task: Write a paragraph. First, pick a side. Agree with the first or the second pig. In your journal, state your opinion:

Writing an opinion is easy as P-I-E!

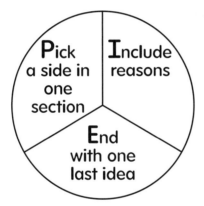

We should build a house of _____

because _____

_____

and _____.

Next, write one last idea to bring your opinion to a close.

LANGUAGE LINK

Opinion Writing

LEARNING SETTING

Individual

DEPTH OF KNOWLEDGE

● ● ● ○

SUPPLIES

Journal, pencil

STANDARD

I can support my opinion with reasons.

LET'S EXPLORE MORE

You Can Write a Terrific Opinion Piece by Jennifer Fandel. You Can Write. North Mankato, MN: Capstone, 2013. (1–2)

Ask the Author

"The End." Slowly, you close the book. Hmm, you still have a few questions about the story. I know! Let's ask the author.

Write a letter to the author:

"Dear _____,"
(Add the author's name.)

Finish the letter. First, write two sentences about yourself. Then, write two questions for the author. Finally, end the letter with one last sentence. This should be a special note to the author. On the next line, write "Thank you," and under it, sign your name.

Ready? Take **5!**

AlphaZoo

All the letters of the alphabet had been placed side by side in a neat row. A, B, C, D. F followed E, and H followed G. On and on the letters went to Z. And then the worst thing happened! Someone did not lock the gate at the local zoo. The animals are escaping. Whoosh! There they go, and there go the letters. The M just flew onto a monkey's back. The G stuck on a goose's beak. Let's get them back together again.

Let's put all the letters into a bag. Now, let's pull a letter from the bag. You got the letter G! What animal could begin with this letter? On the half sheet of paper, draw the animal and the letter. Place the letter anywhere on the animal. Beneath the drawing, write the name of the animal. Any animal will do, even a possamaboo. Never heard of it? Neither have I. But anything is possible at the AlphaZoo!

Put all drawings together in a class book. No one will have a book like this!

Ready? Take

LANGUAGE LINK

Spelling Descriptive Details

LEARNING SETTING

Individual

DEPTH OF KNOWLEDGE

 ● ● ○ ○

SUPPLIES

Bag with letters, half sheets of paper, colored pencils

STANDARDS

I can spell words I don't know by sounding them out.

I can add drawings or details to a description to provide information.

LET'S EXPLORE MORE

Bind the book and provide opportunities for students to read their book to other classes.

The Alphabet Parade by Charles Ghigna. My Little School House. North Mankato, MN: Capstone, 2014. (PreK–2)

SUPPLIES

Journal, pencil, a 10-picture card deck that has a picture of a common object on one side of each card and the name of the object on the back. (Example objects: bridge, popcorn)

STANDARD

I can spell words I don't know by sounding them out.

LET'S EXPLORE MORE

This game can be played again and again as students learn to spell all words correctly. Words and pictures can be changed throughout the year.

Thumbs-up!

Number from 1 to 10 in your journal. Place the deck of cards in the middle of your group's table with all pictures facing up. Look at the first picture. What is the correct spelling? Come to an agreement. Everyone then spells the word by the number 1. Go to the next picture. Talk it out! Then, spell the word beside number 2. Use all the cards in the deck.

Next, turn the deck over. Does the spelling match a word on your list? Yes! Then place a check by the word in your journal. No? Then cross out the word. Spell it correctly on the same line. Count up the checks! How well did your group do?

8 to 10 correct words = thumbs-up

4 to 7 correct words = thumbs sideways

0 to 3 correct words = thumbs-down (but you will do better the next time!)

Ready? Take 5!

Bam!

Pow! Zap! Comic strip heroes use words like these. These sounds are made by heroes and bad guys (also called *villains*). These are "bam!" words. They have an exclamation point after them. This punctuation mark shows their mighty powers.

Use your "Xplain" sheet to create a superhero. It can be a super person, bug, or animal. (Example: Super Ant or Red Wolf) Next, create a villain. He will be the bad guy. Give the villain a name. (Example: The Red Beetle) Draw a story in the spaces. Use "bam!" words. Don't forget the exclamation points. Who will win the battle? The story begins in space 1 and ends in space 4.

Ready? Take

LANGUAGE LINK
Punctuation
Narrative Writing

LEARNING SETTING
Individual

DEPTH OF KNOWLEDGE
● ● ○ ○

SUPPLIES
Journal, colored pencils, "Xplain" Your Writing Graphic Organizer (p. 184)

STANDARDS
I can use end punctuation.

I can write narrative events in the correct order.

LET'S EXPLORE MORE
Use comic books to find more exclamation points.

What Is a Graphic Novel? by Charlotte Guillain. Connect with Text. Chicago, IL: Heinemann Library, 2015. (2–4)

Beginning writers can create simple graphic novels with "Comic Creator" at the ReadWriteThink website.

Advanced writers will enjoy the layers of complexity and choices available for creating their own graphic novel on the Comic Master website.

Go Home!

Go home, Ian! Your mom is calling. Ian lives on Second Street. What about the animals? Where are their homes? Write about or draw the homes for three animals. You may use resources like books or the Internet for help. With a partner, write this on your page:

_____ lives in a _____.

Write the name of the animal in the first blank. In the second blank, write its home.

Example: *A deer lives in a forest.*

Choose three animals from the list below. You can also choose one not on the list.

bees	bats
bears	snails
horses	turtles
ants	beavers
birds	spiders

Next, write two sentences about this home. Add one last sentence:

Everything needs a home because _____.

Ready? Take **5!**

Life in Sunnyville

People loved Sunnyville. This town was once "full" of life and beauty. People were cheerful and helpful. Here, all the flowers were beautiful. All dogs and cats were playful. The strong leaders were powerful. It was a joyful place. But then a strange wind blew across Sunnyville. Everything changed.

The skies and rainbows became colorless. (*Less* means *without*.) The rainbow and skies were without any color. The parks were flowerless. They were *without* any flowers. The leaders felt useless. They had nothing to do. And the children became careless. Sunnyville needs help. Make the town a better place!

Write the next part of the story with a partner. This time, use the suffix *-er* to make words. The suffix *-er* means *more*, like *sweeter*. Use words like *brighter, higher, longer, sharper, smoother, newer, fewer, younger, braver,* or *faster*.

Ready? Take 5!

LANGUAGE LINK
Suffixes

LEARNING SETTING
Pair

DEPTH OF KNOWLEDGE
● ● ● ○

SUPPLIES
Journal, pencil

STANDARD
I can use prefixes and/or suffixes to figure out word meanings.

LET'S EXPLORE MORE

I Am Powerful!: Younger students can use a list of suffixes to describe themselves. This list can contain suffixes such as *-ful, -er, -est,* or *-y.*

Listen to the song "Prefix or Suffix?" by The Bazillions on YouTube.

Spelling
Verbs

Collaborative

DEPTH OF KNOWLEDGE

SUPPLIES

Journal; pencil; stack of five (or more) cards, each with a simple action verb on it: *wink, blink, nod, smile, frown, stretch, lean, sneeze, blow, clap, snap, tap, purr*

STANDARDS

I can spell words I don't know by sounding them out.

I can use verbs.

LET'S EXPLORE MORE

This game can be continued later using other verbs.

Action Words: Verbs by Anita Ganeri. Getting to Grips with Grammar. Chicago, IL: Heinemann Library, 2012. (1–3)

Pass, Catch, Tackle: Football Verbs by Mark Weakland. Football Words. North Mankato, MN: Capstone, 2016. (2–4)

Start clapping with the "Verb Rap Song" by Have Fun Teaching on YouTube.

Wink, Blink, and Nod

It's time for some action! Turn over the first card. It's a verb. It shows action, and so will we! Place the card in the middle of the group. Say the word together ("clap"). Then, spell the word together (C-L-A-P). Then, say the word again, but add the action. Everybody claps three times. Now, turn over another card. It might go like this:

Say: "Wink."

Spell it: "W-I-N-K."

Say it again with the right action: (Wink three times while saying "Wink, wink, wink.")

Keep the action going! Finished? Write these words in your journal. Draw a picture beside each one. Show the action. At the top of the page write "Verbs."

Ready? Take **5!**

On the Road-e-o

Oh, me! What will we see? We'll drive real slow on the road-e-o!

I'm driving to Nog   (short *o* vowel sound)
To see a green frog.

I'm driving to Tote   (long *o* vowel sound)
To see a gray goat.

I'm driving to Deak   (long *e* vowel sound)
To see a giant beak.

I'm driving to Fen   (short *e* vowel sound)
To see a red hen.

Now it's your turn. Where are we going? What will we see? Take along both long and short *i, o,* and *u* vowel sounds. Use the same pattern. With a partner, write three more verses.

....

Ready? Take

LANGUAGE LINK
Spelling Patterns

LEARNING SETTING
Pair

DEPTH OF KNOWLEDGE

SUPPLIES
Journal, pencil

STANDARD
I can write a letter that matches a short vowel and a long vowel sound.

LET'S EXPLORE MORE
Tickles, Pickles, and Floofing Persnickles: Reading and Writing Nonsense Poems by Blake Hoena, Catherine Ipcizade, and Connie Colwell Miller. North Mankato, MN: Capstone, 2014. (2–4)

Many short videos on vowel sounds are available at the PBS Learning Media website.

LANGUAGE LINK
Opinion Writing

LEARNING SETTING
Individual

DEPTH OF KNOWLEDGE

SUPPLIES
Journal, pencil

STANDARD
I can support my opinion with reasons.

LET'S EXPLORE MORE
Beastly Feast by Tracey Corderoy. The Grunt and the Grouch. North Mankato, MN: Capstone, 2013. (1–3)

Create your own duck tale by downloading the "Duck Booklet" from the Activity Village website.

What's for Lunch, Duck?

A duck waddled into the Duck Pond Café.

"What will you have?" the cook asked.

"I will have two bugs, one worm, and four fish eggs."

The cook wrote down the order. "Will that be all?"

"No, add five berries, one frog, and two snails."

The cook looked at duck. "Is there anything you won't eat?"

Well, is there? On your paper, draw a duck pond. Add all the things the duck will eat. Then, add things the duck will not eat. Circle only the foods the duck will eat. Under the picture, complete this sentence:

I will/will not (circle one) join duck for lunch because

_____

_____.

Ready? Take **5!**

Letter Soup Level 1

What's for lunch? It's letter soup! Dip the spoon into the bowl. Pull out four letters. Can you spell a word? Yes? Spell the word on the tray. Put extra letters back into the bowl. Pass the spoon to the left. This player dips into the bowl and pulls four letters. No word? Then hold on to your letters. Keep passing the spoon from one player to the next. After the first round of play, dip in and only take two letters. No more words or letters? The game ends.

Ready? Take

LANGUAGE LINK

Spelling

LEARNING SETTING

Collaborative

DEPTH OF KNOWLEDGE

● ◐ ○ ○

SUPPLIES

One plastic bowl and spoon for each group, magnetic letters and tray

STANDARD

I can spell words I don't know by sounding them out.

LET'S EXPLORE MORE

Letter Soup Level 2: Revisit this prompt another day, but this time add a new element. Players may add to the words already played, like a another popular game and provide an example instead. For example, *cat* plus *s* makes *cats*! At this level, players will want to increase the number of letters in the bowl.

Loads of Letters!: A Spot-It, Learn-It Challenge by Sarah L. Schuette. Spot It, Learn It! North Mankato, MN: Capstone, 2014. (1–2)

Kids can scoop up words in the "Alphabet Soup" game at the PBS Kids website.

LANGUAGE LINK
Spelling Patterns

LEARNING SETTING
Individual

DEPTH OF KNOWLEDGE

SUPPLIES

Journal, pencil

STANDARDS

I can spell simple words by sounding them out.

I can produce complete sentences in class activities.

LET'S EXPLORE MORE

Operation II: Students pair up to operate on another day using four-letter words like *take*.

Doctors Help by Dee Ready. Our Community Helpers. North Mankato, MN: Capstone, 2013. (K–1)

Operation I

Doctor, doctor! Help is needed in room four. We must operate on the word *cat*. Let's operate! First, remove the *c*. Replace it with the letter *b*. Now we have *bat*! Let's operate on the first letter again. Take out the *b* and replace it with *h*. Now we have *hat*. Now, it's your turn.

Write the word *hat* on your paper. Operate on the first letter only. Make a list of new three-letter words that end with *-at*.

Now let's operate on the third letter. Write *cat* at the top of a second list. Remove the *t*. Make a list of new three-letter words that change the last letter. For example, *can*.

Finally, try and operate on the second letter. Write *cat* at the top of the third list. Remove the *a*. Is there another word besides *cot*?

See how well you do with all three lists!

Now, write three sentences. Use one word from each of your three lists.

From list one: The cat lay on the mat.

From list two: Cal wore a cap.

Ready? Take **5!**

Hank's Wish

Hank watched the fish in the glass dish.
He watched it swim around and around.
This looked so easy! So Hank made a wish.
He wished to be a fish in a glass dish.
BAM!
Hank's wish came true!
He now he is a fish, too.
And so Hank swims in a glass tank.
He swims around and around.
But this is too easy! So Hank made a wish.

What does Hank wish? In your journal, copy the rest of the poem and fill in the blanks. What will Hank be next? You might write "He wished to be a lion in a jungle." And "He roars and stalks."

He wished to be a _____ in a _____.

BAM!

Hank's wish came true!

He now is a _____, too.

And so Hank _____ in a _____.

He _____ and _____.

But this is too easy! So Hank made a wish.

He wished to be a _____ in a _____.

Add as many verses as you like! Share with the rest of the class.

Ready? Take 5!

LANGUAGE LINK
Narrative Writing

LEARNING SETTING
Individual

DEPTH OF KNOWLEDGE
● ● ◐ ○

SUPPLIES
Journal, pencil

STANDARD
I can write narrative events in the correct order.

LET'S EXPLORE MORE
This story can be used again at a later time with new adventures for Hank.

I Want to Be … (Series) by Thomas Kingsley Troupe. North Mankato, MN: Capstone, 2016. (K–3)

Frankly, I Never Wanted to Kiss Anybody!: The Story of the Frog Prince as Told by the Frog by Nancy Loewen. The Other Side of the Story. North Mankato, MN: Capstone, 2014. (2–3)

LANGUAGE LINK
Verbs

LEARNING SETTING
Individual

DEPTH OF KNOWLEDGE
● ○ ○ ○

SUPPLIES
Journal, pencil

STANDARD
I can use verbs and nouns that match tense.

LET'S EXPLORE MORE

Owls by Mary R. Dunn. Nocturnal Animals. North Mankato, MN: Capstone, 2012. (PreK–2)

Trust, Truth, and Ridiculous Goofs: Reading and Writing Friendship Poems by Connie Colwell Miller, Blake Hoena, and Jennifer Fandel. Poet in You. North Mankato, MN: Capstone, 2014. (2–4)

Keep the beat going with the "Action Verbs Sing Along" from TeacherTube Studios on YouTube.

Whoo Are Your Friends?

Answer these questions in your journal:

Who tells funny stories? _____

Who runs fast? _____

Who sings songs? _____

Who plays a sport? _____

Write one sentence for each of these verbs: *tells, runs, sings, plays.* Can you write a sentence with two of these verbs? How about three?

Ready? Take **5!**

The Sky Is Falling!

One fall day, Henny Penny said, "The sky is falling!"

"That's not the sky," Turkey Lurkey said. "Those are leaves!"

One winter day, Henny Penny said, "The sky is falling!"

"That's not the sky," Chicken Little said. "That is snow!"

One spring day, Henny Penny said, "The sky is falling!"

"That's not the sky," Goosey Loosey said. "That's just rain!"

One summer day, Henny Penny said, "The sky is falling!"

"That's not the sky," Ducky Lucky said. "Those are sunbeams!"

Henny Penny needs help. In each plain, or space, on your "Xplain" sheet, write the name of each season: fall, winter, spring, and summer. Then, answer this question: How can Henny Penny enjoy each season? Draw Henny Penny having fun in each of the four seasons. Below each picture, write a sentence. Describe what Henny Penny is doing.

Ready? Take

LEARNING SETTING
Individual

DEPTH OF KNOWLEDGE

SUPPLIES

Journal, colored pencils, "Xplain" Your Writing Graphic Organizer (p. 184)

STANDARDS

I can write narrative events in the correct order.

I can add drawings or details to a description to provide information.

LET'S EXPLORE MORE

Seasons Come and Seasons Go by Bruce Bednarchuk. Cantata Learning. North Mankato, MN: Capstone, 2015. (1–3)

True or False? Seasons by Daniel Nunn. Seasons. Chicago, IL: Heinemann Library, 2013. (PreK–1)

SUPPLIES

Journal, pencil

STANDARD

I can support my opinion with reasons.

LET'S EXPLORE MORE

Use this prompt again with different subjects like a bird and cat or a fish and flower.

Basil the Bear Cub by Janey Louise Jones. Superfairies. North Mankato, MN: Capstone, 2016. (K–3)

I Want to Be … (Series) by Thomas Kingsley Troupe. North Mankato, MN: Capstone, 2016. (K–3)

The Bear or the Bee

A bear   or   a bee?

Which would you be? List three reasons. Write this in your journal:

I would be a _____ because

_____

_____

_____.

Ready? Take

The Talking Toy Box

One night each year, the toys come alive. What will they say? Write one sentence for each toy.

Toy Bear said, "_____

_____."

Princess Doll said, "_____

_____."

Rocket Man said "_____

_____."

Ready? Take 5!

LANGUAGE LINK
Complete Sentences

LEARNING SETTING
Individual

DEPTH OF KNOWLEDGE
● ◯ ◯ ◯

SUPPLIES
Journal, pencil

STANDARD
I can produce complete sentences in class activities.

LET'S EXPLORE MORE
Encourage students to work with other verbs like *cried, shouted, questioned, stated,* or *replied.* On another day, a prompt could have the toys talk to one another.

Princess Heart (Series) by Molly Martin. North Mankato, MN: Capstone, 2013. (PreK–1)

Students will enjoy creating fun stories with "Story Maker" at the British Council's LearnEnglish Kids website.

LANGUAGE LINK
Opinion Writing

LEARNING SETTING
Individual

DEPTH OF KNOWLEDGE

SUPPLIES

Journal, pencil

STANDARD

I can support my opinion with reasons.

LET'S EXPLORE MORE

Michael Dahl's Really Scary Stories (Series) by Michael Dahl. North Mankato, MN: Capstone, 2016. (2–3)

Would You Ever?

Would you pet a snake?
Would you sleep with a tiger?
Would you eat a bumblebee?
Would you dance with a bear?

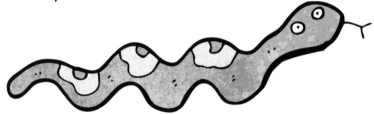

Finish each sentence.

I would never _____

because _____

_____.

I would never _____

because _____

_____.

I would never _____

because _____

_____.

Share your "I would never" sentences with the class.

Ready? Take

Mood Ring

Shyla's feeling a bit silly. D'Sean is feeling a bit down. Tanya is nervous. She has a test today. Tomorrow, Tanya will be very happy. Her test will be over. Have you ever felt silly, sad, or nervous? These are called *moods*.

You can go from sad to mad to happy all in one day! Draw a ring on your paper with one large stone. This is a mood ring. The color of the stone shows your mood. Pink could mean happy. Orange could mean happy. What's your mood? Choose one of these twelve moods.

funny	safe	happy	afraid	nervous	lazy
shy	sad	silly	strong	angry	excited

Next, select a color for this mood. Color the stone in that color. Under the ring, complete this sentence:

I sometimes feel _____

because _____

_____.

Name of a famous person: _____
(Examples: The President, a singer, a baseball or football player, George Washington, the Tin Man, the Queen of England) probably feels or felt _____

because _____

_____.

Ready? Take 5!

LANGUAGE LINK
Opinion Writing

LEARNING SETTING
Individual

DEPTH OF KNOWLEDGE

SUPPLIES
Journal, pencil, colored pencils

STANDARD
I can support my opinion with reasons.

LET'S EXPLORE MORE
The Grumpy Lobster by Cari Meister. Stone Arch Readers. North Mankato, MN: Capstone, 2013. (2–4)

Explore "Many Moods" with Thomas the Tank Engine at the PBS Kids website.

What Did You See at the Sea?

What are the sights and sounds of the forest, the city, and the seaside? You visited the forest last week. You are in the city today. Tomorrow, you will go to the seaside. The verbs can move through time. They show the past, the present, and the future. Complete each sentence with your ideas.

Yesterday I heard a _____ in the forest.

I also heard a _____.

Today I see a _____ in the city.

I also see a _____.

Today I hear a _____ in the city.

I also hear _____.

Tomorrow I will see _____ at the seaside.

I will also see _____.

Tomorrow I will hear _____ at the seaside.

I will also hear _____.

Ready? Take **5!**

Shh! Don't Wake Buddy!

Buddy is your dog. Listen. He is growling in his sleep. He is shaking all over. Is he sick? No! Buddy is having a bad dream.

Draw Buddy in his bed. Next, draw a large circle above his head. Draw Buddy's dream in this circle.

Under the picture, explain his dream. Begin with this sentence:

Buddy is scared. He is dreaming of _____.

···

Ready? Take

LANGUAGE LINK
Narrative Writing

LEARNING SETTING
Individual

DEPTH OF KNOWLEDGE
● ○ ○ ○

SUPPLIES

Journal, pencil

STANDARD

I can write narrative events in the correct order.

LET'S EXPLORE MORE

Students can continue the adventures of Buddy in their own stories.

A Dog's Day by Rebecca Rissman. Chicago, IL: Heinemann Library, 2014. (1–2)

Little Sister

Nicki has always wanted a sister. And today her wish will come true. Nicki and her parents adopted a little girl and brought her home. Her new sister is five years old. Her name is Mei. It sounds like "May." Nicki has another wish. She wants to be a very good sister. What can she do? List four things a big sister or big brother can do.

1. _____

   _____

2. _____

   _____

3. _____

   _____

4. _____

   _____

Ready? Take **5!**

Hop on Board!

Get a move on! The bus is waiting. This bus makes six stops.

- Stop one: ice-cream shop

- Stop two: bike shop

- Stop three: school

- Stop four: playground

- Stop five: grocery store

- Stop six: mall

You have three stops today. What will you do?

At stop _____, I will _____.

At stop _____, I will _____.

At stop _____, I will _____.

Ready? Take

LANGUAGE LINK
Narrative Writing

LEARNING SETTING
Individual

DEPTH OF KNOWLEDGE

● ○ ○ ○

SUPPLIES

Journal, pencil

STANDARD

I can write narrative events in the correct order.

LET'S EXPLORE MORE

Students can extend this activity by drawing one of the bus stops and themselves in the picture.

Wheels on the Bus by Steven Anderson. Sing-Along Songs. North Mankato, MN: Cantata Learning, 2016. (1–3)

LANGUAGE LINK
Informative Writing

LEARNING SETTING
Individual

DEPTH OF KNOWLEDGE

SUPPLIES

Journal, pencil

STANDARDS

I can provide supporting details for a topic in informative writing.

LET'S EXPLORE MORE

Grow Your Own Smoothie by John Malam. Grow It Yourself! Chicago, IL: Heinemann Library, 2012. (K–2)

Energy Drink

Whir! Marlen is helping her mother. She is putting vegetables into the blender. Marlen and her mom are making an energy drink together. First, Marlen tosses in spinach, carrots, nuts, apple chunks, lemon juice, honey, and coconut water. She then hits the button again. Whir! It is ready! Slurp!

Now it is your turn. What would make a good energy drink? Write five items in your journal. How will you make it? List the steps to make your energy drink. Then, answer this question: Why would this energy drink be good for you?

Ready? Take 5!

Whose Hat Is That?

Cowboys wear hats. Firemen do too. But what about you? What kind of hat suits you? On your paper, draw three hats. They should be very different. Next, circle the hat for you. Under the drawing, write this sentence:

I would wear THIS hat because _____

_____.

Ready? Take **5!**

LANGUAGE LINK
Opinion Writing

LEARNING SETTING
Individual

DEPTH OF KNOWLEDGE

● ● ● ○

SUPPLIES
Journal, pencil

STANDARD
I can support my opinion with reasons.

LET'S EXPLORE MORE

Book-O-Hats: A Wearable Book by Donald Lemke. A Wearable Book. North Mankato, MN: Capstone, 2015. (PreK–1)

Pick a Picture, Write an Opinion! by Kristen McCurry. Little Scribe. North Mankato, MN: Capstone, 2014. (1–2)

LANGUAGE LINK
Spelling

LEARNING SETTING
Individual

DEPTH OF KNOWLEDGE

SUPPLIES
Journal, pencil

STANDARD
I can spell words by using spelling patterns.

LET'S EXPLORE MORE

Farmer Jones Rides Again: On another day, students can rearrange their words and place them in sentences by including additional words.

Farmer in the Dell by Steven Anderson. Sing-Along Songs. North Mankato, MN: Cantata Learning, 2016. (1–3)

Grouping Words: Sentences by Anita Ganeri. Getting to Grips with Grammar. Chicago, IL: Heinemann Library, 2012. (1–3)

Farmer Jones

Farmer Jones and his truck are heading to the market. He is so tired. He has picked words all day. They are now piled into the back of his truck.

BUMP! Off they go. What was that? Farmer Jones just hit a big bump in the road. All the words have fallen out! They are all broken! Help Mr. Jones put the words back together again. Here are the letters. No letters can be used twice. Write down each word on your page.
Try to find the longest word. Look carefully! Some are capital letters!

a	b	g	e	t	S	m
R	e	a	L	i	o	s
f	a	n	y	e	p	r
O	W	r	T	a	y	i
u	k	F	M	a	c	o

Ready? Take

Appendices

Alphabetical Index of Prompts

Prompt	Language Link	CCSS: K	CCSS: 1st	CCSS: 2nd	Page
The Colors of the Rainbow	Sorting	L.K.5.A	L.1.5.A	L.2.5	32
Color Squares	Sorting	L.K.5.A	L.1.5.A	L.2.5	37
Coming Soon!	Research	W.1.7	W.1.7	W.2.7	109
Daffy Definitions	Compound Words	L.K.5	L.1.4	L.2.4.D	80
A Day at the Beach	Opinion Writing	W.K.1	W.1.1	W.2.1	48
A Day at the Zoo	Descriptive Writing	SL.K.4	SL.1.4	SL.2.4	21
Dinnertime in the Forest	Spelling Patterns Opinion Writing	L.K.2.C W.K.1	L.1.2.D W.1.1	L.2.2.D W.2.1	28
Do You See What I See?	Descriptive Writing	SL.K.4	SL.1.4	SL.2.4	34
Duck!	Opinion Writing	W.K.1	W.1.1	W.2.1	33
Easy as PIE	Opinion Writing	W.K.1	W.1.1	W.2.1	141
Eek! It's a Mouse!	Descriptive Writing	L.K.1	L.1.1.F	L.2.1.E	55
Energy Drink	Informative Writing	W.K.2	W.1.2	W.2.2	164
Farmer Jones	Spelling	L.K.2.D	L.1.2.D	L.2.2.D	166
Farmer Jones Rides Again	Sentences	L.K.1.F	L.1.1.J	L.2.1.F	166
Fear in the Forest	Plural Nouns	L.K.1.C	L.1.1	L.2.1	50
Freaky Fruit	Descriptive Writing	SL.K.4	SL.1.4	SL.2.4	62
Future Cars	Opinion Writing	W.K.1	W.1.1	W.2.1	63
Give Me a Hand!	Descriptive Writing	SL.K.4	SL.1.4	SL.2.4	133
Go Home!	Research	W.1.7	W.1.7	W.2.7	146
Hank's Wish	Narrative Writing	W.K.3	W.1.3	W.2.3	153
A Helpful Dinosaur	Narrative Writing	W.K.3	W.1.3	W.2.3	85
Help! Police!	Synonyms Adjectives	L.K.5 L.K.1	L.1.5.D L.1.1.F	L.2.5 L.2.1.E	83
Hey, Taxi!	Capitalization	L.K.2	L.1.2	L.2.2	76
Honeybees	Informative Writing	W.K.2	W.1.2	W.2.2	24
Hop on Board!	Narrative Writing	W.K.3	W.1.3	W.2.3	163
How Do You Do That?	Informative Writing	W.K.2	W.1.2	W.2.2	139
How to Ride an Elephant	Informative Writing	W.K.2	W.1.2	W.2.2	139
I Am Powerful!	Suffixes	SL.K.4	SL.1.4	SL.2.4	147
I See Colors	Sorting	L.K.5.A	L.1.5.A	L.2.5	123
I See Shapes	Sorting	L.K.5.A	L.1.5.A	L.2.5	123
Kid-in-Space	Narrative Writing	W.K.3	W.1.3	W.2.3	86
Kings Bree and McFee	Antonyms	L.K.5.B	L.1.5	L.2.5	41

Prompt	Language Link	CCSS: K	CCSS: 1st	CCSS: 2nd	Page
Leap Frog	Spelling Patterns Opinion Writing	L.K.2.C W.K.1	L.1.2.D W.1.1	L.2.2.D W.2.1	28
Let's Go!	Prepositions Nouns	L.K.1.E L.K.1.B	L.1.1.I L.1.1.B	L.2.1 L.2.1	35
Letter Bingo	Sorting	L.K.5.A	L.1.5.A	L.2.5	88
Letter Detectives	Complete Sentences Spelling Patterns	L.K.1.F L.K.2	L.1.1.J L.1.2.D	L.2.1.F L.2.2.D	93
Letter Soup Level 1	Spelling	L.K.2.D	L.1.2.D	L.2.2.D	151
Letter Soup Level 2	Spelling	L.K.2.D	L.1.2.D	L.2.2.D	151
Letter Swap	Spelling Patterns	L.K.2.D	L.1.2.D	L.2.2.D	42
Life in Sunnyville	Suffixes	L.K.4.B	L.1.4.B	L.2.4.C	147
Little Sister	Informative Writing	W.K.2	W.1.2	W.2.2	162
The Lonely Duck	Narrative Writing	W.K.3	W.1.3	W.2.3	33
The Long Train Ride	Opinion Writing	W.K.1	W.1.1	W.2.1	125
Lost and Found	Apostrophes	L.K.1	L.1.1.B	L.2.2.C	97
The Lost Elf	Narrative Writing	W.K.3	W.1.3	W.2.3	25
Lost Pooch	Descriptive Writing	SL.K.4	SL.1.4	SL.2.4	78
Lucy's Puppies	Capitalization	L.K.2	L.1.2	L.2.2	38
Lunch with a Sea Lion	Narrative Writing	W.K.3	W.1.3	W.2.3	114
Macee's Big Mess	Spelling Capitalization	L.K.2 L.K.2.A	L.1.2.D L.1.2	L.2.2.D L.2.2	90
Make a Pattern	Sorting	L.K.5.A	L.1.5.A	L.2.5	120
Martin's Dream	Descriptive Writing	SL.K.4	SL.1.4	SL.2.4	121
Match Game	Verb Agreement	L.K.1	L.1.1.C	L.2.1	67
Me First!	Opinion Writing	W.K.1	W.1.1	W.2.1	56
Missing Sounds	Spelling Patterns Complete Sentences	L.K.2.D L.K.1.F	L.1.2.D L.1.1.J	L.2.2.D L.2.1.F	119
Mixed-up Art	Descriptive Writing	SL.K.4	SL.1.4	SL.2.4	124
The Mixed-up Elephant	Descriptive Writing	SL.K.5	SL.1.5	SL.2.5	131
Mood Ring	Opinion Writing	W.K.1	W.1.1	W.2.1	159
Mr. Clover's Fruit Stand	Adjectives	L.K.1	L.1.1.F	L.2.1.E	122
Mr. Flip Flap	Narrative Writing	W.K.3	W.1.3	W.2.3	71
My Pet Obo	Descriptive Writing	SL.K.4	SL.1.4	SL.2.4	77
My School	Capitalization	L.K.2.A	L.1.2	L.2.2	92

Prompt	Language Link	CCSS: K	CCSS: 1st	CCSS: 2nd	Page
The Neighbors of Building C	Opinion Writing	W.K.1	W.1.1	W.2.1	103
Not Again!	Prefixes Informative Writing	L.K.4.B W.K.2	L.1.4.B W.1.2	L.2.4.B W.2.2	138
Object Art	Opinion Writing	W.K.1	W.1.1	W.2.1	99
The Octopus	Sentences	L.K.1.F	L.1.1.J	L.2.1.F	126
Oh No, Terrick!	Sentences	L.K.1.F	L.1.1.J	L.2.1.F	127
On the Road-e-o	Spelling Patterns	L.K.2.C	L.1.2.D	L.2.2.D	149
Operation I	Spelling Patterns	L.K.2.D	L.1.2.D	L.2.2.D	152
Operation II	Spelling Patterns	L.K.2.D	L.1.2.D	L.2.2.D	152
Our School Campus	Capitalization	L.K.2	L.1.2	L.2.2	76
Party Time!	Informative Writing	W.K.2	W.1.2	W.2.2	112
Peace	Descriptive Writing	SL.K.5	SL.1.5	SL.2.5	121
A Peachy Preposition	Prepositions Narrative Writing	L.K.1.E W.K.3	L.1.1.I W.1.3	L.2.1 W.2.3	45
The Perfect Tree House	Descriptive Writing	SL.K.4	SL.1.4	SL.2.4	113
Pete the Pelican	Verbs	L.K.1.B	L.1.1.E	L.2.1	29
Pet Names	Capitalization	L.K.1.A	L.1.1.A	L.2.2	30
Pick up the Phone!	Opinion Writing	W.K.1	W.1.1	W.2.1	94
Picture Stories	Narrative Writing	W.K.3	W.1.3	W.2.3	128
Picture the Animals	Descriptive Writing	SL.K.4	SL.1.4	SL.2.4	36
Picture This	Descriptive Writing	SL.K.4	SL.1.4	SL.2.4	34
Pizza Bar	Sorting	L.K.5.A	L.1.5.A	L.2.5	70
Playtime in the Den	Informative Writing.	W.K.2	W.1.2	W.2.2	107
The Pool Adventure	Narrative Writing	W.K.3	W.1.3	W.2.3	68
Puppy Doctor	Informative Writing	W.K.2	W.1.2	W.2.2	51
The Quiet Thief	Plural Nouns	L.K.1	L.1.1	L.2.1.B	49
Raven's Present	Descriptive Writing	SL.K.4	SL.1.4	SL.2.4	101
Recycling	Opinion Writing	W.K.1	W.1.1	W.2.1	24
Red, Yellow, Purple Lights	Narrative Writing	W.K.3	W.1.3	W.2.3	104
The Rest of the Story	Research	W.1.7	W.1.7	W.2.7	46
The River Town Rat Race	Narrative Writing	W.K.3	W.1.3	W.2.3	132
The Root Word Game	Root Words Suffixes	L.K.4 L.K.4.B	L.1.4.C L.1.4.B	L.2.4.C L.2.4.C	129
The Runaway Sock I	Descriptive Writing	SL.K.4	SL.1.4	SL.2.4	136

Prompt	Language Link	CCSS: K	CCSS: 1st	CCSS: 2nd	Page
The Runaway Sock II	Narrative Writing	W.K.3	W.1.3	W.2.3	136
Saturday Morning	Descriptive Writing	SL.K.4	SL.1.4	SL.2.4	25
Say Cheese!	Interrogatives	L.K.1.D	L.1.1	L.2.1	128
School Bus Safety	Informative Writing	W.K.2	W.1.2	W.2.2	104
The Science Museum	Informative Writing	W.K.2	W.1.2	W.2.2	21
Shh! Don't Wake Buddy!	Narrative Writing	W.K.3	W.1.3	W.2.3	161
The Sinking Boat	Pronouns	L.K.1	L.1.1.D	L.2.1	66
The Sky Is Falling!	Narrative Writing Descriptive Details	W.K.3 SL.K.5	W.1.3 SL.1.5	W.2.3 SL.2.5	155
The Sleeping Giant I	Antonyms Adjectives	L.K.5.B L.K.1	L.1.5 L.1.1.F	L.2.5 L.2.1.E	101
The Sleeping Giant II	Narrative Writing	W.K.3	W.1.3	W.2.3	101
SNAP!	Antonyms	L.K.5.B	L.1.5	L.2.5	130
Space Party	Informative Writing	W.K.2	W.1.2	W.2.2	112
Splat, Rip, and Roar	Narrative Writing	W.K.3	W.1.3	W.1.3	40
Step into the Painting	Narrative Writing	W.K.3	W.1.3	W.2.3	98
A Story in Pictures	Narrative Writing	W.K.3	W.1.3	W.2.3	108
The Strange Bug	Descriptive Writing	SL.K.4	SL.1.4	SL.2.4	87
A Summer Day I	Narrative Writing Synonyms	W.K.3 L.K.5	W.1.3 L.1.5.D	W.2.3 L.2.5	118
A Summer Day II	Narrative Writing Synonyms	W.K.3 L.K.5	W.1.3 L.1.5.D	W.2.3 L.2.5	118
Superstars	Capitalization	L.K.2	L.1.2.A	L.2.2.A	110
The Talking Toy Box	Complete Sentences	L.K.1.F	L.1.1.J	L.2.1.F	157
Team Spirit	Descriptive Writing	SL.K.4	SL.1.4	SL.2.4	102
Tessa's Present	Narrative Writing	W.K.3	W.1.3	W.2.3	96
That's a Bunch!	Collective Nouns	L.K.1	L.1.1	L.2.1.A	111
This Is Me! 1	Informative Writing Descriptive Details	W.K.2 SL.K.5	W.1.2 SL.1.5	W.2.2 SL.2.5	57
This Is Me! 2	Informative Writing Descriptive Details	W.K.2 SL.K.5	W.1.2 SL.1.5	W.2.2 SL.2.5	58
This Is Me! 3	Opinion Writing Descriptive Details	W.K.1 SL.K.5	W.1.1 SL.1.5	W.2.1 SL.2.5	59
This Is MY School	Research	W.1.7	W.1.7	W.2.7	134
Thumbs-up!	Spelling	L.K.2.D	L.1.2.E	L.2.2.D	144

Prompt	Language Link	CCSS: K	CCSS: 1st	CCSS: 2nd	Page
Timeline	Narrative Writing	W.K.3	W.1.3	W.2.3	65
Treasure or Trash?	Sorting Opinion Writing	L.K.5.A W.K.1	L.1.5.A W.1.1	L.2.5 W.2.1	52
True or False	Prefixes	L.K.4.B	L.1.4.B	L.2.4.B	31
Unrhymed Poetry Time	Spelling Patterns Complete Sentences	L.K.2.D L.K.1.F	L.1.2.D L.1.1.J	L.2.2.D L.2.1.F	119
Valentine Cards	Descriptive Details	SL.K.5	SL.1.5	SL.2.5	140
Veggie Scramble	Sorting Opinion Writing	L.K.5.A W.K.1	L.1.5.A W.1.1	L.2.5 W.2.1	84
The Very Busy Day	Narrative Writing	W.K.3	W.1.3	W.2.3	89
The Very Verby Vacation	Verbs	L.K.1	L.1.1.E	L.2.1	43
A Walk in the Park	Antonyms	L.K.5.B	L.1.5	L.2.5	73
Watch Out, Nate!	Prepositions Narrative Writing	L.K.1.E W.K.3	L.1.1.I W.1.3	L.2.1 W.2.3	45
Welcome Home!	Apostrophes Formal vs. Informal Writing	L.K.2 N/A	L.1.2 N/A	L.2.2.C L.2.3.A	81
What an Ending!	Punctuation	L.K.2.B	L.1.2.B	L.2.2	72
What Did You See at the Sea?	Verbs	L.K.1.B	L.1.1.E	L.2.1.D	160
What's for Dinner?	Adjectives Plural Nouns	L.K.1 L.K.1.C	L.1.1.F L.1.1	L.2.1.E L.2.1	54
What's for Lunch, Duck?	Opinion Writing	W.K.1	W.1.1	W.2.1	150
What's New at the Zoo?	Descriptive Writing	SL.K.4	SL.1.4	SL.2.4	36
What's the Big Idea?	Informative Writing	W.K.2	W.1.2	W.2.2	27
Where's Mirle?	Narrative Writing	W.K.3	W.1.3	W.2.3	83
Where's Wendy?	Prepositions	L.K.1.E	L.1.1.I	L.2.1	53
Whoo Are Your Friends?	Verbs	L.K.1.8	L.1.1.E	L.2.1	154
Whose Hat Is That?	Opinion Writing	W.K.1	W.1.1	W.2.1	165
Who Stole the Pie?	Punctuation	L.K.2.B	L.1.2.B	L.2.2	115
Who Wants Pizza?	Opinion Writing	W.K.1	W.1.1	W.2.1	21
Wiggle Worm, Wiggle Worm	Narrative Writing	W.K.3	W.1.3	W.2.3	82
Will You Be My Valentine?	Informative Writing	W.K.2	W.1.2	W.2.2	140
Wink, Blink, and Nod	Spelling Verbs	L.K.2.D L.K.1	L.1.2.D L.1.1.E	L.2.2.D L.2.1	148
Wishing on a Star	Opinion Writing	W.K.1	W.1.1	W.2.1	116

Prompt	Language Link	CCSS: K	CCSS: 1st	CCSS: 2nd	Page
A Wrinkled Twinkle Rhyme	Spelling Patterns	L.K.2.D	L.1.2.D	L.2.2.D	60
The "Write" Way to Fish	Writing Process	Anchor Standard CCRA.W.4, W.5			19
Word Bump	Compound Words	L.K.5	L.1.4	L.2.4.D	80
Would You Ever?	Opinion Writing	W.K.1	W.1.1	W.2.1	158
Write a "Re" Story	Narrative Writing	W.K.3	W.1.3	W.2.3	138

Bibliography

Albuquerque Public Schools (2016). "Webb's Depth of Knowledge Guide." Retrieved November 12, 2015 from http://www.aps.edu/re/documents/resources/Webbs_DOK_Guide.pdf.

Atwell, N. M. (1998). *In the middle: New understandings about writing, reading, and learning (2nd ed.).* Portsmouth, NJ: Heinemann.

Berninger, V., Rutberg, J., Abbott, R., Garcia, N., Anderson-Youngstrom, M., Brooks, A. & Fulton, C. (2006). Tier 1 and tier 2 early intervention for handwriting and composing. *Journal of School Psychology, 44(1),* 3–30.

Bratcher, S. (2009). *The learning to write process in elementary classrooms.* New York: Routledge.

Calkins, L. (1994). *The art of teaching writing.* Portsmouth, NH: Heinemann.

Graham, S., Bollinger, A., Booth Olson, C., D'Aoust, C., MacArthur, C., McCutchen, D. & Olinghouse, N. (2012). *Teaching elementary school students to be effective writers: A practice guide* (NCEE 2012-4058). Washington, DC: National Center for Education Evaluation and Regional Assistance, Institute of Education Sciences, U.S. Department of Education. Retrieved November 12, 2015 from http://ies.ed.gov/ncee/wwc/publications_reviews.aspx#pubsearch.

Graham, S., Harris, K. & Fink, B. (2000). Is handwriting causally related to learning to write? Treatment of handwriting problems in beginning writers. *Journal of Educational Psychology, 92(4),* 620–633.

Graham, S. and Hebert, M. (2010). *Writing to read: Evidence for how writing can improve reading.* Washington, DC: Alliance for Excellence in Education.

Graham, S., Harris, K. & Fink-Chorzempa, B. (2002). Contribution of spelling instruction to the spelling, writing, and reading of poor spellers. *Journal of Educational Psychology, 94(4),* 669–686.

Graham, S., MacArthur, C.A. & Fitzgerald, J. (2013). *Best practices in writing instruction (2nd Ed.).* New York: Guilford.

Graves. D. H. (1994). *A fresh look at writing.* Portsmouth, NH: Heinemann.

Johnston, P. (2012). *Opening minds: Using language to change lives.* Portland, ME: Stenhouse.

Moss, C. M., S. M. Brookhart, and B. A. Long. (2011). "Knowing Your Learning Target." *Educational Leadership,* 68(6), 66–69. Retrieved October 17, 2015 from http://www.ascd.org/publications/educational-leadership/mar11/vol68/num06/Knowing-Your-Learning-Target.aspx

National Association for the Education of Young Children (1998). Learning to read and write: Developmentally appropriate practices for young children. *Young Children,* 53 (4), 30–46.

National Council of Teachers of English. (2016). NCTE beliefs about the teaching of writing.

National Governors Association Center for Best Practices & Council of Chief State School Officers (2010). *Common Core State Standards for English language arts and literacy in history/social studies, science, and technical subjects.* Washington, DC: Authors.

Saddler, B. & Asaro-Saddler, K. (2009). Writing better sentences: Sentence-combining instruction in the classroom. *Preventing School Failure, 54(3),* 159–163.

Salahu-Din, D., Persky, H. & Miller, J. (2008). *The nation's report card: Writing 2007* (NCES#2008-468). Washington, DC: National Center for Education Statistics, Institute of Education Sciences, U.S. Department of Education. Retrieved November 12, 2015 from the National Center for Education Statistics website: http://nces.ed.gov/nationsreportcard/pdf/main2007/2008468.pdf

Tracy, B., Reid, R. & Graham, S. (2009). Teaching young students strategies for planning and drafting stories: The impact of self-regulated strategy development. *Journal of Educational Research, 102(5),* 323–331.

Yarrow, F. & Topping, K. (2001). Collaborative writing: The effects of metacognitive prompting and structured peer interaction. *British Journal of Educational Psychology, 71,* 261–282.

Zimmerman, B. J. (2001). Theories of self-regulated learning and academic achievement: An overview and analysis. In B. J. Zimmerman & D. H. Schunk (Eds.), *Self-regulated learning and academic achievement: Theoretical perspectives* (pp. 1–65). Mahwah, NJ: Erlbaum.

Master List of Children's Books Referenced

Action Words: Verbs by Anita Ganeri. Getting to Grips with Grammar. Chicago, IL: Heinemann Library, 2012. (1–3)

Adventure Stories by Anita Ganeri. Writing Stories. Chicago, IL: Heinemann Library, 2014. (1–3)

The Alphabet Parade by Charles Ghigna. My Little School House. North Mankato, MN: Capstone, 2014. (PreK–2)

The Amazing Adventures of Superman! Battle of the Super Heroes! by Yale Stewart. DC Super Heroes. North Mankato, MN: Capstone, 2015. (K–2)

Amazing Elephants by Charlotte Guillain. Walk on the Wild Side. Chicago, IL: Heinemann Library, 2014. (2–4)

Animals by Charlotte Guillain. Jobs If You Like .... Chicago, IL: Heinemann Library, 2013. (1–3)

Animals All Day! (Series) by Joanne Ruelos Diaz. North Mankato, MN: Capstone, 2015. (K–2)

Animals That Live in Groups by Kelsi Turner Tjernagel. Learn about Animal Behavior. North Mankato, MN: Capstone, 2013. (1–2)

Art by Charlotte Guillain. Jobs If You Like .... Chicago, IL: Heinemann Library, 2013. (1–3)

Art-Rageous by Jessica Young. Finley Flowers. North Mankato, MN: Capstone, 2016. (2–3)

Basil the Bear Cub by Janey Louise Jones. Superfairies. North Mankato, MN: Capstone, 2016. (K–3)

Beach Bummer by Michele Jakubowski. Perfectly Poppy. North Mankato, MN: Capstone, 2014. (K–2)

Beastly Feast by Tracey Corderoy. The Grunt and the Grouch. North Mankato, MN: Capstone, 2013. (1–3)

Before and After by Joy Frisch-Schmoll. Exploring Opposites. North Mankato, MN: Capstone, 2013. (K–1)

Bingo by Steven Anderson. Sing-Along Songs. North Mankato, MN: Cantata Learning, 2016. (PreK–3)

Book-O-Hats: A Wearable Book by Donald Lemke. A Wearable Book. North Mankato, MN: Capstone, 2015. (PreK–1)

California Sea Lions by Megan C. Peterson. Marine Mammals. North Mankato, MN: Capstone, 2013. (K–1)

Captain Kidd's Crew Experiments with Sinking and Floating by Mark Weakland. North Mankato, MN: Capstone, 2012. (2–3)

A Cat Is Chasing Me Through This Book by Benjamin Bird. Tom and Jerry. North Mankato, MN: Capstone, 2015. (PreK–2)

Celebrating Differences (Series) by Melissa Higgins. North Mankato, MN: Capstone, 2012. (K–1)

City Train by Adria F. Klein. Train Time. North Mankato, MN: Capstone, 2013. (PreK–1)

Colorful World of Animals (Series) by Mandy R. Marx and Cecilia Pinto McCarthy. North Mankato, MN: Capstone, 2012. (K–1)

Coppernickel Goes Mondrian by Wouter van Reek. Brooklyn, NY: Enchanted Lion Books, 2012. (PreK–3)

Describing Words: Adjectives, Adverbs, and Prepositions by Anita Ganeri. Getting to Grips with Grammar. Chicago, IL: Heinemann Library, 2012. (1–3)

Dinosaurs: Can You Tell the Facts from the Fibs? by Kelly Liner Halls. Lie Detector. North Mankato, MN: Capstone, 2016. (K–3)

Doctors Help by Dee Ready. Our Community Helpers. North Mankato, MN: Capstone, 2013. (K–1)

The Doggone Dog by Diana G. Gallagher. Pet Friends Forever. North Mankato, MN: Capstone, 2014. (1–3)

A Dog's Day by Rebecca Rissman. Chicago, IL: Heinemann Library, 2014. (1–2)

Drawing Pets: A Step-By-Step Sketchbook by Mari Bolte. My First Sketchbook. North Mankato, MN: Capstone, 2015. (1–2)

The Duckster Ducklings Go to Mars: Understanding Capitalization by Nancy Loewen. Language on the Loose. North Mankato, MN: Capstone, 2016. (2–4)

Eddie and Ellie's Opposites (Series) by Daniel Nunn. Chicago, IL: Heinemann Library, 2014. (PreK–K)

Elephants Are Awesome! by Martha E. H. Rustad. Awesome African Animals! North Mankato, MN: Capstone, 2015. (1–2)

Exploring Space (Series) by Martha E. H. Rustad. North Mankato, MN: Capstone, 2012. (K–1)

The Fancy Octopus by Cari Meister. Stone Arch Readers. North Mankato, MN: Capstone, 2012. (2–3)

Farmer in the Dell by Steven Anderson. Sing-Along Songs. North Mankato, MN: Cantata Learning, 2016. (1–3)

Fingerprint Bugs by Bobbie Nuytten. Fun with Fingerprints. North Mankato, MN: Capstone, 2016. (K–1)

Flip-Side Nursery Rhymes (Series) by Christopher Harbo. North Mankato, MN: Capstone, 2015. (PreK–2)

Frankly, I Never Wanted to Kiss Anybody!: The Story of the Frog Prince as Told by the Frog by Nancy Loewen. The Other Side of the Story. North Mankato, MN: Capstone, 2014. (2–3)

Frog. Frog? Frog!: Understanding Sentence Types by Nancy Loewen. Language on the Loose. North Mankato, MN: Capstone, 2014. (2–4)

Funny Stories by Anita Ganeri. Writing Stories. Chicago, IL: Heinemann Library, 2014. (1–3)

Fun Things to Do with Cardboard Tubes by Marne Ventura. 10 Things to Do. North Mankato, MN: Capstone, 2015. (1–2)

Fun Things to Do with Paper Cups and Plates by Kara L. Laughlin. 10 Things to Do. North Mankato, MN: Capstone, 2015. (1–2)

Games Around the World by Clare Lewis. Around the World. Chicago, IL: Heinemann Library, 2015. (PreK–1)

Grouping Words: Sentences by Anita Ganeri. Getting to Grips with Grammar. Chicago, IL: Heinemann Library, 2012. (1–3)

Grow Your Own Smoothie by John Malam. Grow It Yourself! Chicago, IL: Heinemann Library, 2012. (K–2)

The Grumpy Lobster by Cari Meister. Stone Arch Readers. North Mankato, MN: Capstone, 2013. (2–4)

A Hat Full of Adjectives by Bette Blaisdell. Words I Know. North Mankato, MN: Capstone, 2014. (1–2)

Henri's Scissors by Jeanette Winter. New York, NY: Beach Lane Books, 2013. (K–3)

Henry Helps with the Baby by Beth Bracken. Henry Helps. North Mankato, MN: Capstone, 2012. (PreK–K)

How Books Are Made by Martha E. H. Rustad. Wonderful World of Reading. North Mankato, MN: Capstone, 2013. (K–1)

How to Read a Map by Melanie Waldron. Let's Get Mapping! Chicago, IL: Heinemann Library, 2013. (2–4)

I Can Write Letters and E-Mails by Anita Ganeri. I Can Write. Chicago, IL: Heinemann Library, 2013. (1–3)

In and Out by Joy Frisch-Schmoil. Exploring Opposites. North Mankato, MN: Capstone, 2013. (K–1)

Insects by Martha E. H. Rustad. Smithsonian Little Explorer. North Mankato, MN: Capstone, 2015. (1–2)

It Doesn't Need to Rhyme, Katie Woo by Fran Manushkin. Katie Woo: Star Writer. North Mankato, MN: Capstone, 2014. (K–2)

I Want to Be … (Series) by Thomas Kingsley Troupe. North Mankato, MN: Capstone, 2016. (K–3)

Joining Words: Conjunctions by Anita Ganeri. Getting to Grips with Grammar. Chicago, IL: Heinemann Library, 2012. (1–3)

Jobs If You Like … (Series) by Charlotte Guillain. Chicago, IL: Heinemann Library, 2013. (1–3)

Kylie Jean Party Craft Queen by Marci Peschke and Marne Ventura. Kylie Jean Craft Queen. North Mankato, MN: Capstone, 2014. (2–3)

Learning About Poems by Martha E. H. Rustad. North Mankato, MN: Capstone, 2015. (K–1)

Little Red Riding Duck by Charlotte Guillain. Animal Fairy Tales. Chicago, IL: Heinemann Library, 2013. (PreK–2)

Loads of Letters!: A Spot-It, Learn-It Challenge by Sarah L. Schuette. Spot It, Learn It! North Mankato, MN: Capstone, 2014. (1–2)

Look Inside a Bee Hive by Megan C. Peterson. Look Inside Animal Homes. North Mankato, MN: Capstone, 2012. (PreK–2)

Look Inside Animal Homes (Series) by Megan C. Peterson. North Mankato, MN: Capstone, 2012. (PreK–2)

Manners at Home by Sian Smith. Oh, Behave! Chicago, IL: Heinemann Library, 2013. (PreK–1)

Maps, Maps, Maps! by Kelly Boswell. Displaying Information. North Mankato, MN: Capstone, 2014. (1–2)

Martha the Little Mouse by Janey Louise Jones. Superfairies. North Mankato, MN: Capstone, 2016. (K–3)

Martin Luther King Jr. by Riley Flynn. Great African-Americans. North Mankato, MN: Capstone, 2014. (K–1)

Mice Capades by Diana G. Gallagher. Pet Friends Forever. North Mankato, MN: Capstone, 2015. (1–3)

Michael Dahl's Really Scary Stories (Series) by Michael Dahl. North Mankato, MN: Capstone, 2016. (2–3)

The Missing Mouse by Jacqueline Jules. Sofia Martinez. North Mankato, MN: Capstone, 2015. (K–2)

Monsters Can Mosey: Understanding Shades of Meaning by Gillia M. Olson. Language on the Loose. North Mankato, MN: Capstone, 2014. (2–4)

A Mouthful of Onomatopoeia by Bette Blaisdell. Words I Know. North Mankato, MN: Capstone, 2014. (1–2)

My Dog Is as Smelly as Dirty Socks: And Other Funny Family Portraits by Hanoch Piven. New York, NY: Dragonfly Books, 2012. (PreK–3)

My Hometown by Russell Griesmer. North Mankato, MN: Capstone, 2016. (1–4)

Nature Calls by Jessica Young. Finley Flowers. North Mankato, MN: Capstone, 2016. (2–3)

A Nature Walk on the Beach by Richard Spilsbury and Louise Spilsbury. Nature Walks. Chicago, IL: Heinemann Library, 2015. (K–2)

The Noisy Paint Box: The Colors and Shapes of Kandinsky's Abstract Art by Barb Rosenstock. New York, NY: Knopf Books for Young Readers, 2014. (1–4)

Octopuses by Anna Claybourne. Animal Abilities. Chicago, IL: Heinemann Library, 2014. (2–4)

Original Recipe by Jessica Young. Finley Flowers. North Mankato, MN: Capstone, 2016. (2–3)

Owls by Mary R. Dunn. Nocturnal Animals. North Mankato, MN: Capstone, 2012. (PreK–2)

The Parts of a Book by Martha E. H. Rustad. Wonderful World of Reading. North Mankato, MN: Capstone, 2013. (K–1)

Pass, Catch, Tackle: Football Verbs by Mark Weakland. Football Words. North Mankato, MN: Capstone, 2016. (2–4)

Passenger Trains by Nikki Bruno Clapper. All Aboard! North Mankato, MN: Capstone, 2016. (K–1)

Patterns Outside by Daniel Nunn. Math Every Day. Chicago, IL: Heinemann Library, 2012. (PreK–K)

Photographs by Isabel Thomas. Start with Art. Chicago, IL: Heinemann Library, 2012. (K–2)

Pick a Picture, Write an Opinion! by Kristen McCurry. Little Scribe. North Mankato, MN: Capstone, 2014. (1–2)

Pick a Picture, Write a Poem! by Kristen McCurry. Little Scribe. North Mankato, MN: Capstone, 2014. (1–2)

Poppy's Puppy by Michele Jakubowski. Perfectly Poppy. North Mankato, MN: Capstone, 2015. (K–2)

Princess Heart (Series) by Molly Martin. North Mankato, MN: Capstone, 2013. (PreK–1)

Punctuation: Commas, Periods, and Question Marks by Anita Ganeri. Punctuation. Chicago, IL: Heinemann Library, 2012. (1–3)

Rain, Rain, Go Away by Steven Anderson. Tangled Toons. North Mankato, MN: Cantata Learning, 2016. (1–3)

Reading Is Everywhere by Martha E. H. Rustad. Wonderful World of Reading. North Mankato, MN: Capstone, 2013. (K–1)

Scooby-Doo's Color Mystery by Benjamin Bird. Scooby-Doo! North Mankato, MN: Capstone, 2015. (PreK–K)

Seasons Come and Seasons Go by Bruce Bednarchuk. My First Science Songs. North Mankato, MN: Cantata Learning, 2015. (1–3)

Shapes Are Everywhere! by Charles Ghigna. My Little School House. North Mankato, MN: Capstone, 2014. (PreK–2)

A Short History of Valentine's Day by Sally Lee. Holiday Histories. North Mankato, MN: Capstone, 2016. (K–1)

Should Charlotte Share?: Being a Good Friend by Rebecca Rissman. What Would You Do? Chicago, IL: Heinemann Library, 2013. (PreK–1)

Show Me Dinosaurs: My First Picture Encyclopedia by Janet Riehecky. My First Picture Encyclopedias. North Mankato, MN: Capstone, 2013. (1–2)

Sincerely, Katie: Writing a Letter with Katie Woo by Fran Manushkin. Katie Woo: Star Writer. North Mankato, MN: Capstone, 2014. (K–2)

Sing-Along Silly Songs (Series) by Steven Anderson. North Mankato, MN: Cantata Learning, 2016. (1–3)

Special Forces by Ellen Labrecque. Heroic Jobs. Chicago, IL: Heinemann Library, 2012. (1–2)

Spelling Queen by Marci Peschke. Kylie Jean. North Mankato, MN: Capstone, 2012. (2–3)

Squirrels by Mari Schuh. Backyard Animals. North Mankato, MN: Capstone, 2015. (K–1)

Stick to the Facts, Katie: Writing a Research Paper with Katie Woo by Fran Manushkin. Katie Woo: Star Writer. North Mankato, MN: Capstone, 2014. (K–2)

Superman Colors by Benjamin Bird. DC Comics. North Mankato, MN: Capstone, 2015. (PreK–1)

Taking a Trip: Comparing Past and Present by Rebecca Rissman. Comparing Past and Present. Chicago, IL: Heinemann Library, 2014. (PreK–1)

There's a Mouse Hiding in This Book! by Benjamin Bird. Tom and Jerry. North Mankato, MN: Capstone, 2014. (PreK–2)

Thesaurus Rex by Michael Dahl. Library of Doom: The Final Chapters. North Mankato, MN: Capstone, 2016. (1–3)

They're Up to Something in There: Understanding There, Their, and They're by Cari Meister. Language on the Loose. North Mankato, MN: Capstone, 2016. (2–4)

Thorns, Horns, and Crescent Moons: Reading and Writing Nature Poems by Connie Colwell Miller and Jennifer Fandel. Poet in You. North Mankato, MN: Capstone, 2014. (2–4)

Thumbtacks, Earwax, Lipstick, Dipstick: What Is a Compound Word? by Brian P. Cleary. Minneapolis, MN: Millbrook Press, 2013. (2–3)

Tickles, Pickles, and Floofing Persnickles: Reading and Writing Nonsense Poems by Blake Hoena, Catherine Ipcizade, and Connie Colwell Miller. North Mankato, MN: Capstone, 2014. (2–4)

Timelines, Timelines, Timelines! by Kelly Boswell. Displaying Information. North Mankato, MN: Capstone, 2014. (1–2)

Transportation Zone (Series) by Peter Brady. North Mankato, MN: Capstone, 2012. (1–2)

True or False? Seasons by Daniel Nunn. Seasons. Chicago, IL: Heinemann Library, 2013. (PreK–1)

Trust, Truth, and Ridiculous Goofs: Reading and Writing Friendship Poems by Connie Colwell Miller, Blake Hoena, and Jennifer Fandel. Poet in You. North Mankato, MN: Capstone, 2014. (2–4)

Twinkle, Twinkle Little Star by Megan Borgert-Spaniol. Sing-Along Songs. North Mankato, MN: Cantata Learning, 2015. (1–3)

U.S. Military Forces (Series) by Michael Green. North Mankato, MN: Capstone, 2013. (1–2)

Vegetables by Nancy Dickmann. Healthy Eating with MyPlate. Chicago, IL: Heinemann Library, 2012. (PreK–1)

Veterinarians Help by Dee Ready. Our Community Helpers. North Mankato, MN: Capstone, 2013. (K–1)

We All Do Something Well by Shelley Rotner. Shelley Rotner's World. North Mankato, MN: Capstone, 2013. (1–2)

We All Look Different by Melissa Higgins. Celebrating Differences. North Mankato, MN: Capstone, 2012. (K–1)

Welcome to the Treehouse by Art Baltzar and Franco. DC Comics Tiny Titans. North Mankato, MN: Capstone, 2013. (1–2)

What Can Live at the Beach? by John-Paul Wilkins. What Can Live There? Chicago, IL: Heinemann Library, 2015. (PreK–1)

What Do You Think, Katie?: Writing an Opinion Piece with Katie Woo by Fran Manushkin. Katie Woo: Star Writer. North Mankato, MN: Capstone, 2014. (K–2)

What Happens Next, Katie?: Writing a Narrative with Katie Woo by Fran Manushkin. Katie Woo: Star Writer. North Mankato, MN: Capstone, 2014. (K–2)

What Is a Conjunction? by Jennifer Fandel. Parts of Speech. North Mankato, MN: Capstone, 2013. (K–1)

What Is a Family? by Rebecca Rissman. Families. Chicago, IL: Heinemann Library, 2012. (PreK–1)

What Is a Graphic Novel? by Charlotte Guillain. Connect with Text. Chicago, IL: Heinemann Library, 2015. (2–4)

What Is an Adjective? by Jennifer Fandel. Parts of Speech. North Mankato, MN: Capstone, 2013. (K–1)

What Is a Preposition? by Sheri Doyle. Parts of Speech. North Mankato, MN: Capstone, 2013. (K–1)

What Is a Pronoun? by Sheri Doyle. Parts of Speech. North Mankato, MN: Capstone, 2013. (K–1)

Whatever says mark: Knowing and Using Punctuation by Terry Collins. Language on the Loose. North Mankato, MN: Capstone, 2014. (2–4)

What's with the Long Naps, Bears? by Thomas Kingsley Troupe. The Garbage Gang's Super Science Questions. North Mankato, MN: Capstone, 2016. (K–2)

Wheels on the Bus by Steven Anderson. Sing-Along Songs. North Mankato, MN: Cantata Learning, 2016. (1–3)

Who Can Fly? by Cody McKinney. Animal World. North Mankato, MN: Cantata Learning, 2015. (1–3)

Whoosh, Crunch, Roar: Football Onomatopoeia by Mark Weakland. Football Words. North Mankato, MN: Capstone, 2016. (2–4)

Whose Home Is This? by Julie Murphy. Nature Starts. North Mankato, MN: Capstone, 2012. (1–2)

The Wizard of Oz Colors by Jill Kalz. The Wizard of Oz. North Mankato, MN: Capstone, 2014. (1–2)

Words I Know (Series) by Bette Blaisdell. North Mankato, MN: Capstone, 2014. (1–2)

Writing Stories (Series) by Anita Ganeri. Chicago, IL: Heinemann Library, 2014. (1–3)

Yogi Bear's Guide to Bugs by Mark Weakland. Yogi Bear's Guide to the Great Outdoors. North Mankato, MN: Capstone, 2016. (1–2)

You Can Write a Terrific Opinion Piece by Jennifer Fandel. You Can Write. North Mankato, MN: Capstone, 2013. (1–2)

"Xplain" Your Writing Graphic Organizer

A plain is a large open field. An "Xplain" is a very large "X" on your paper. It makes four open writing plains, or spaces. You can then EXPLAIN and organize your ideas. Write or draw one idea in each plain. Move from the top down to the right.

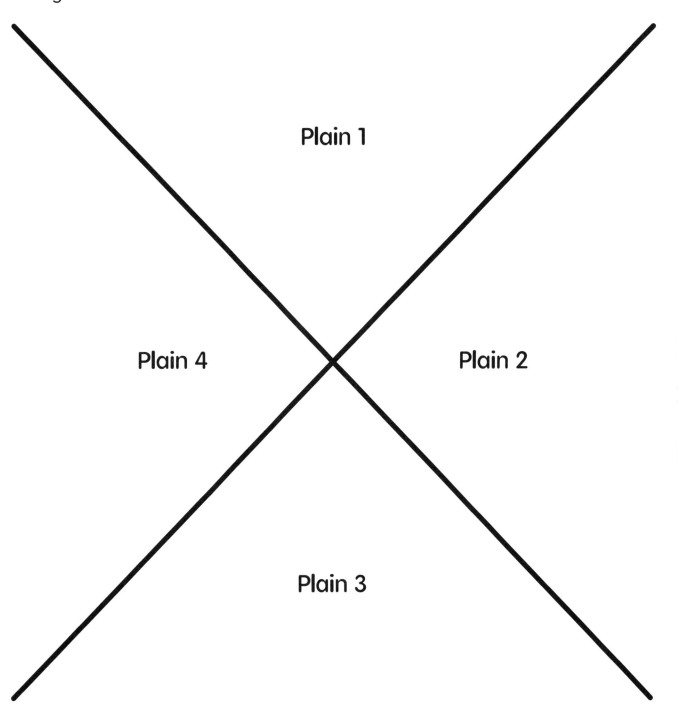

Plain 1

Plain 4

Plain 2

Plain 3

This Is Me! Body Template

Use with the following prompts: This Is Me! 1 on page 57, This Is Me! 2 on page 58, and This Is Me! 3 on page 59.

A Writer's Checklist

_____ 1. Think of many topics. Choose one.

_____ 2. Brainstorm for details. List them.

_____ 3. Write your story. Focus on content.

_____ 4. Read your story aloud. Listen.

_____ 5. Make changes. Add or take away.

_____ 6. Write the story again.

_____ 7. Let others read your story.

_____ 8. Edit and revise.

_____ 9. Write one last time and share!

My Writing Page

Name: _____

I am writing about

_____

It looks like this.

Let's Write About

Name _____

Topic: _____

Purpose: _____

    Informative   Narrative   Opinion   Descriptive

Main Idea: _____

_____

_____

_____

Detail or Reason 1	Detail or Reason 2	Detail or Reason 3
_____	_____	_____
_____	_____	_____
_____	_____	_____
_____	_____	_____
_____	_____	_____

Conclusion: _____

_____

ABC Writing Chart

Aa Bb Cc Dd

Ed Ff Gg Hh

Ii Jj Kk Ll Mm

Nn Oo Pp Qq

Rr Ss Tt Uu Vv

Ww Xx Yy Zz

1 2 3 4 5 6 7 8 9 0

Peer Conference Guide

Star Writers

 Read with a pencil in hand.

 Listen to suggestions.

 Are willing to make changes.

Star Listeners

 Stay focused on the story.

 Make helpful suggestions.

 Respond with positive praise.

Journal Rubric for Developing Writers

Journal Rubric

☀	⛅	🌧	⛈
Wow! Very clear writing	Nice but a little cloudy at times	Many unclear responses	Crash! What was this?
Answered all parts of the prompt	Answered most parts of the prompt	Did not finish all of the prompt	Did not answer the prompt
Ideas were very clever and unique	Ideas were interesting	Ideas were a bit confusing	Ideas were hidden from the reader
Clearly understood language links	Understood most language links	More help needed with language links	Much help needed with language links
Very detailed responses	Most responses had good details	Mostly short responses	Yes. No. That's about it.

Journal Rubric for Beginning Writers

Circle or color one starfish.
Which one best describes your writing?

I need help!

I can begin using more capital letters.

I can begin using more end markings with sentences.

I can begin using more correctly spelled words.

I can begin keeping my ideas from running together.

I can focus more and try harder.

I did my very best!

I can begin sentences with capital letters.

I can use end markings, or punctuation.

I can spell most of my words correctly.

I can stretch my thinking and my words!

I can organize my writing.

I did a good job!

I can begin most sentences with capital letters.

I can use end markings for most sentences.

I can spell most of my words correctly.

I can stretch my thinking more and use new words.

I can organize most of my ideas.

For: _____

Maupin House
capstone

At Maupin House by Capstone Professional, we continue to look for professional development resources that support grades K–8 classroom teachers in areas, such as these:

Literacy	*Language Arts*
Content-Area Literacy	*Research-Based Practices*
Assessment	*Inquiry*
Technology	*Differentiation*
Standards-Based Instruction	*School Safety*
Classroom Management	*School Community*

If you have an idea for a professional development resource, visit our Become an Author website at:
http://www.capstonepub.com/classroom/professional-development/become-an-author

There are two ways to submit questions and proposals.

1. You may send them electronically to:
   proposals@capstonepd.com

2. You may send them via postal mail. Please be sure to include a self-addressed stamped envelope for us to return materials.

Acquisitions Editor
Capstone Professional
1 N. LaSalle Street, Suite 1800
Chicago, IL 60602